An Apology
for Poetry

The Library of Liberal Arts

SIR PHILIP SIDNEY

An Apology
for Poetry

Edited, with an Introduction and notes, by
FORREST G. ROBINSON
Assistant Professor of English
Harvard University

The Library of Liberal Arts
published by
Macmillan Publishing Company
New York
Collier Macmillan Publishers
London

Sir Philip Sidney: 1554–1586

Macmillan Publishing Company
866 Third Avenue
New York, New York, 10022

First Edition
Ninth Printing — 1987

Library of Congress Catalog Card Number: 73-122682
Designed by Starr Atkinson

ISBN 0-02-402560-7

Contents

Introduction

LIFE AND MAJOR WORKS

The narrative of Sidney's life is a study in great, and greatly frustrated, expectations.[1] Although born into potentially enormous wealth and power, he was on the verge of poverty for most of his adult life and became a knight only when court protocol made it inevitable; and although scrupulously groomed as a courtier and statesman, he had only sporadic and imperfect successes with a queen whose temperament and political situation demanded more calculated prudence, and less idealism, than he could offer. Even his death, while remembered as an example of great personal heroism, served no important military objective and was the result of careless bravado in the name of a frustrated and ultimately unsuccessful political adventure. His literary reputation, great as it was in his own time, and great as it is today, was of little concern to Sidney. His major works were the fruits of enforced idleness, of periods when "politic" Elizabeth (perhaps wisely) gave him little to do, or banished him from the court altogether. Indeed, had he had his way, Sidney would be ranked with men like Leicester and Burghley and Essex, and not with Spenser and Shakespeare.

Sidney was born on November 30, 1554. As a first son he was

[1]Biographical details have been gathered from Malcolm William Wallace, *The Life of Sir Philip Sidney* (1915); Roger Howell, *Sir Philip Sidney, The Shepherd Knight* (1968); and Fulke Greville, *Life of Sir Philip Sidney*, ed. Nowell Smith (1907).

heir to the power and position that descended from both branches of his family. His father, Sir Henry Sidney, Elizabeth's Lord Governor in Ireland for many years, and one of her least rewarded though most devoted and qualified servants, was the only son of Sir William Sidney, who rose to eminence during the reign of Henry VIII. Lady Mary, Philip's mother, was the daughter of John Dudley, the once powerful Duke of Northumberland. Lady Mary's family remained tremendously influential in the second half of the sixteenth century, even though her father, an ambitious promoter of the Protestant cause during the reign of Edward VI, had gone to the scaffold for treason in 1553. This influence rested largely with her brother, Robert Dudley, later the Earl of Leicester, perhaps the only man that the queen ever loved passionately. Handsome, gallant, cultured, athletic, and the head of the Puritan contingent among the royal advisers, Leicester was too strong and too radical to sit comfortably behind Elizabeth on the throne. For many years it appeared that young Philip would someday fall heir to his uncle's great fortune and prestige. But Sidney's premature death and the earl's unexpected marriage combined to nullify promising appearances. In the English political arena, however, Leicester's encouragement and example were important to his nephew's development. Sidney's subsequent support of the Protestant cause in the Netherlands, his aggressive attitude toward Spain, and the frustration at court that these views entailed, were the mixed blessing that his uncle conferred upon him.

Of Sidney's early life we know very little. Since his father was in Ireland much of the time, the responsibility for supervising the household and arranging for her son's education must have fallen to Lady Mary. In his tenth year, however, Sidney left Penshurst, the family home, and entered Shrewsbury School, situated on the banks of the Severn in Shropshire County. The school was a model of its kind, marshaling about four hundred boys through a predominantly Latin curriculum which included Cicero, Caesar, Sallust, Livy, Virgil, Horace, Ovid, and Terence. There was also a modicum of training in Greek, notably Isocrates and Xenophon, though it is unlikely that Sidney ever achieved real competence in this language. The reputation of the school was largely attributable to the eminence of its headmaster, Thomas Ashton, whose strong Puritan bias was a formative influence on the students who came within his purview. And in this model school Sidney seems to have been a model, if perhaps painfully earnest, student. His lifelong friend and classmate at Shrewsbury, Fulke Greville, later wrote of him: "Though I lived with him, and knew him from a child, yet I never knew him other than a man: with such staidnesse of mind, lovely, and familiar gravity, as carried grace, and reverence above greater years. His talk ever of knowledge, and his very play tending to enrich his mind."[2]

In the late summer of 1566 Sidney, now approaching his twelfth birthday, abandoned his school work for a short time in order to visit the Earl of Leicester at Kenilworth Castle. No doubt he made the journey with enthusiasm, for in addition to seeing his most powerful relative, his itinerary included a trip to Oxford, where Leicester was the newly installed chancellor, and where the queen was scheduled to sojourn for several days in the midst of elaborate celebrations. After nearly a week at Kenilworth, Sidney set out for Oxford with a sumptuous new suit which his uncle had ordered for him. It proved appropriate to the occasion. The queen's visit at the university commenced with a spectacular procession of dignitaries, the exchange of flamboyant compliments, opulent gifts, and the first of many Latin orations. All was pomp and dignified high spirits. The queen entered in an open chariot drawn by magnificently decorated horses, her regal demeanor, her jewels, her sovereignty obvious to everyone present. No doubt the events of that afternoon, and of the week that followed, sent Sidney back to Shrewsbury with a profound sense of the power and grandeur that were his own great expectations.

About a year after his first visit to Oxford Sidney returned, this time to matriculate at Christ Church. Of this period we

[2]*Life of Sir Philip Sidney*, p. 6.

know little, except that he was on good terms with one of Leicester's most formidable adversaries, Sir William Cecil, later Elizabeth's trusted Lord Burghley. In fact, relations were so close that in 1569 it was assumed that he would marry Cecil's daughter, Anne. A settlement was duly drawn up, but by 1570 there had been a misunderstanding, and the match was off. We can be sure that Sidney was powerless to alter the marital course that his elders charted for him, and so this early failure can hardly have been a personal one. Given his studious temperament, it seems rather likely that his enthusiasms were intellectual rather than romantic during the three or four years that he spent at the university. Grammar, rhetoric, and logic formed the center of an Oxford education, and these disciplines were presented with characteristically humanistic reverence for the classics. There are also indications that Sidney excelled in the undergraduate disputations, scholastic debates designed to test the student's knowledge and to improve his Latin. Academic prowess notwithstanding, however, and for reasons that are far from clear, Sidney left Oxford without a degree in 1571. It may be that he was at Cambridge for a while, in which case he would have had an opportunity to meet Edmund Spenser and Gabriel Harvey.

In any case, by 1572 Sir Henry, with Leicester's encouragement, had decided to send his son abroad. The journey was obviously designed as the final stage in the grooming of a courtier and statesman, for it would allow Sidney to perfect his already considerable skill in foreign languages, and it would expose him to the delicate balance of continental powers. Accordingly, late in the spring he made his first stop in Paris, there to remain for three months in the home of Sir Francis Walsingham, the ambassador to France and later his father-in-law. In the course of this brief stay Sidney had two experiences that were instrumental in forming the patterns of his later life. First, among his various acquaintances with prominent French leaders (Admiral Coligny, Peter Ramus, perhaps Phillipe de Mornay and Michel de l'Hôpital) he numbered Hubert Languet, a learned and respected advocate of European Protestantism. Perhaps because of his advanced years, Languet took an almost paternal interest in Sidney; he encouraged him in his education, arranged introductions with prominent scholars and political figures, and later offered prudent counsel when his protégé had returned to the English court. Their mutual affection, and Languet's guiding influence, are evident in the long and spirited correspondence which persisted almost until the old man's death in 1581.[3]

The second of the critical events in Paris was the infamous Massacre of St. Bartholomew. What happened, briefly, was this. The French crown was torn between two powerful factions. The king, Charles IX, was a spineless weakling, but nevertheless sympathetic to the Protestant cause, and a friend of Coligny, the leader of the Huguenots. But the family of the king, led notably by Catherine de' Medici, was opposed to the Protestant faction, and made every effort to divert the king's sympathies. Suddenly, in August 1572, Coligny was assassinated. Charles foolishly submitted to the advice of Catherine, who persuaded him that the Huguenots were ready to take arms against his throne. Convinced that his power was in jeopardy, the king decided to protect himself. What ensued was one of the blackest episodes in French history. The streets of Paris were virtually littered with the corpses of thousands of Huguenots who were hunted down and slaughtered. Sidney must have observed the brutal spectacle from the safety of Walsingham's house, where he was no doubt horrified by what he saw, and confirmed in his mistrust of Roman Catholics.

The remainder of Sidney's stay in Europe was happily less exciting, but no less interesting, than the few weeks that he spent in France. In October he traveled north to Frankfurt, and there, under the watchful eye of Languet, spent the winter studying and conversing with his mentor's friends. In the early spring of 1573 he journeyed to Heidelberg, met Henry Stephens, the famous printer-scholar, and then moved on to Strassburg, where

[3]See *The Correspondence of Sir Philip Sidney and Hubert Languet*, ed. S. A. Pears (1845).

he was entertained by another eminent humanist, John Sturm. After these brief stops he made his way to the Imperial Court in Vienna, where Languet was performing his duties as the ambassador for the Elector of Saxony. An excursion to Hungary and several months in Vienna left Sidney anxious to get on with his travels, this time to Italy. Languet was uneasy about the plan, and understandably so, since sixteenth-century Protestants looked upon Italy as the Babylon of Europe, a whirlpool of Machiavellian corruption and Popish excess. But Sidney would have his way. For the better part of a year Languet fretted with worry while his impetuous young friend journeyed to Venice, to Padua, to Florence, before returning to Vienna for the winter of 1574. In the early spring of the following year he made his farewell with Languet and moved slowly westward across the continent. By the end of May he was in Antwerp boarding the ship that would carry him, three years older and decades wiser, back to England.

It would be difficult to overestimate the importance of Sidney's continental tour. The precepts of Languet's humanism, which marshaled classical learning into an alignment with Protestant politics, were admirably illustrated in the gallery of scholars and political leaders who impressed, and were impressed by, his protégé from England. Little wonder that for the rest of his life it was Sidney's most pressing ambition to support the interests of Protestantism in Europe. But, as he must have realized almost immediately upon his return to England, the road to power and influence ran through the court of a queen whose policies promised to frustrate his own.

In spite of obvious hazards, however, Sidney's first two or three years at court were cause for some optimism. Not long after his return he was a guest at a spectacular entertainment which Leicester presented for the queen at Kenilworth. We can well imagine that Elizabeth, encouraged by the occasion, cast a favorable eye on the earl's impressive young nephew, for in the following year Sidney became her cupbearer. During the same period Sidney probably visited Ireland, where his father was serving as Lord Governor. Here, while observing the impossible conditions that his father had to cope with, he became friendly with the aging Earl of Essex, another of the queen's viceroys in Ireland. Not long after Sidney's arrival the old earl died, though not before he voiced the hope that his young friend would join his daughter in marriage. In the course of handling the dead earl's affairs Sidney may have met young Penelope Devereux, but we can be fairly sure that he was initially unmoved by the girl who was to become the Stella of his sonnets The prospect of matrimony could have had little appeal for a courtier whose main interests and objectives were more and more bound up with political developments on the continent. William of Orange, the leader of the Protestant revolt against Spain in the Netherlands, had only recently appealed to Elizabeth to assume control of his country. Sidney and Leicester were probably enthusiastic about the proposal, for it would involve England in an aggressive policy against Spain, and it would support the cause of Protestantism. But the queen, whose paramount concern was to keep the European powers at each other's throats, and hence away from hers, realized that antagonisms between France and Spain over the Netherlands would probably cease if she agreed to Orange's plan. Her position was complicated by the Duke of Alençon, the younger brother of the king of France, who had abandoned the French court and taken command of a Huguenot army. Alençon was making a bid for Elizabeth's hand, no doubt to compound his own power, but Elizabeth saw that such a marriage would alienate the French crown, and might lead to an alliance between France and Spain. Accordingly her policy, almost certainly the right one, consisted in encouraging Orange and leading Alençon along, without formally committing herself to either. The difference between her stance and that of Leicester's party, which amounted to the difference between political realism and impractical idealism, was to remain unchanged almost until the end of Sidney's life.

Their latent conflicts notwithstanding, in 1577 the queen sent Sidney on a state journey to the continent. In the company of his friends Fulke Greville and Edward Dyer, Sidney made his way to Germany, where it was his ostensible mission to offer the queen's condolences for deaths in the families of certain German princes. In fact, the primary objective of the journey was to gain a more intimate acquaintance with the political climate in Germany, and in this the queen's ambassador seems to have been successful. But the most stirring event of the trip was a meeting with William of Orange. As a result of Sidney's ready sympathy for his position, Orange commissioned the Englishman to renew his offer of an alliance with England. Not unexpectedly, the proposal was turned down, but the occasion itself was crucial in confirming Sidney's allegiance to the Netherlands, and in establishing once and for all his differences with the queen.

Sidney's return to England marked the beginning of a period of bustling activity. Toward the end of 1577 he wrote a *Discourse of Irish Affairs* in defense of his father's activities in Ireland. At the same time he was investing considerable sums of money in the voyages of Martin Frobisher, though these never paid off, and simply intensified the pressure of his financial worries. In the spring of 1578 his pastoral entertainment, *The Lady of May*,[4] was presented to the queen when she visited Leicester at Wanstead. But the main business of his life soon became the Alençon match, which had surfaced as an ugly possibility in 1578 and had become a probability by the following year. Elizabeth toyed with the proposal, though she was probably simply equivocating in order to gain time, and never took the Frenchman, who was half her age, very seriously. But she was convincing enough to provoke many of her subjects, including Sidney, who, probably with Leicester's encouragement, wrote a long letter to the queen arguing that the marriage was doomed to failure, that Alençon was a weakling, even worse, a Frenchman, and that the English public would not have it. This was commendably honest, but

[4]Where there are uncertainties in dating Sidney's works, and there are several, I have followed Ringler's conclusions in *Poems*.

hardly diplomatic. Elizabeth's subsequent decision to abandon the plans for marriage was in no way inspired by Sidney's letter, which had its most important result in its author's exile from court.

For the next four or five years Sidney was forced to settle for a comparatively minor role in the entourage of a determined queen. His public activities were limited to a couple of terms in Parliament, participation in a number of chivalric tournaments, and a journey to the Netherlands with Leicester. In January of 1583 he stood as proxy for his old friend Count Casimir of Germany, who was installed *in absentia* as a Knight of the Garter. Sidney was knighted in order to meet the requirements of his role in the ceremony, but the perfunctory title can have done little to raise his spirits. Indeed, the brightest event in these years of frustrated ambitions and financial decline was Sir Philip's marriage, in September 1583, to Frances Walsingham, the daughter of Sir Francis Walsingham, one of Leicester's most powerful allies. The marriage was fruitful in more ways than one. It seems to have been a happy union; it produced Sidney's only child, Elizabeth; and it cinched up already firm ties with the Leicester faction.

Sidney may not have agreed, but from our point of view the most positive result of his exile from court was that it forced him into the role of a poet. By the end of the summer of 1580, after an extended visit with his sister Mary, the Countess of Pembroke, he had completed the original or what is known as the *Old Arcadia*. Patterned after a work of the same name by the Italian poet Sannazzaro, the original *Arcadia* is a prose romance with verse eclogues punctuating its five books. Sidney presented the manuscript to his sister and occupied himself with other things until sometime shortly before or in 1584, when he embarked on a major revision of his original. Although the recasting got no further than the middle of the third book, the incomplete *New Arcadia* is much longer than the complete *Old Arcadia*, and radically different in tone and intention. Sidney

fleshed out his romance with a variety of sub-plots, each designed to illustrate moral and political vices and virtues, and
lending the revision an episodic and sententious quality almost
totally lacking in the earlier version. Years later Fulke Greville
reflected that in the *New Arcadia* it was his old friend's design
"to turn the barren Philosophy precepts into pregnant Images
of life."[5]

While reserving the general discussion of *An Apology for
Poetry* for a few moments, we may note that it was composed
at about the same time as *Astrophil and Stella*, between 1581 and
1583. The first of the important Elizabethan sonnet sequences,
Astrophil and Stella fathered a generation of sonneteers, among
whom Daniel, Drayton, Spenser, and Shakespeare rank as the
most distinguished. Its 108 sonnets and 11 songs are a frustrated
narrative of passionate and unfulfilled love, of heroic allegiances
fractured into amorous idleness, of virtue buckling under the
weight of desire, all rendered in tones that modulate from high
Petrarchan elegance to direct colloquial simplicity. Astrophil
was created in the image of his maker, and Stella is almost certainly Penelope, the daughter of Essex, and unhappily the bride
of a fraction of a man, Lord Rich. The autobiographical ele-
ments in the sequence are unquestionable, though Sidney's
veracity in particular details will always remain a tantalizing mys-
tery. Of the merit of the poetry, however, there can be little
doubt. In a genre where he has had few equals, Sidney made
the sonnet into a taut, dramatic medium, compressing infinite
riches in a little room.

In 1585, after more than a little maneuvering behind the
scenes, Sidney's personal fortunes took a turn for the better. In
July of that year he was promoted to Mastership of the Ord-
nance, an office which he shared with his uncle, the Earl of War-
wick. At almost the same time that he received this lucrative
new position, Sidney was no doubt pleased to observe that the
winds of change in Europe were whipping up a crisis that made

[5]*Life of Sir Philip Sidney*, p. 15.

Leicester's policy of active intervention almost inevitable. The French, probably in awe of Spain, had refused to assume the role of protector in the Netherlands, and for Elizabeth this meant the renewed threat of a strong coalition between France and Spain. Accordingly, it became increasingly important to consolidate her unity with the Protestant forces in the Low Countries. In spite of grave reservations, she initiated negotiations with her allies and resolved to send military support across the channel. As Malcolm Wallace observes, her decision "was tantamount to a declaration of war with Spain."[6] At first uncertain about his place in the enterprise, and probably vexed at the queen's delays, Sidney almost ruined his chances for military service by organizing a secret expedition to the New World with Sir Francis Drake. But the plan collapsed at the last minute when Drake lost his faith in his partner's sea legs, and when the queen discovered what her recalcitrant courtier had in mind. In due time Sidney was restored to favor and appointed Elizabeth's governor in Flushing, a strategic fortress on the coast of the Netherlands.

In mid-November 1585, Sidney set sail for Flushing with his brother Robert and a small group of attendants. Leicester arrived in December to command the operations and, in total disregard for the queen's orders, almost immediately became Governor General of the provinces. During the year that he was actively engaged in the war, Sidney distinguished himself for his courage, his military expertise, and his brilliant leadership. But in September of 1586 Fate, and perhaps his own rash judgment, brought Sidney face to face with disaster. With a band of less than 600 brave comrades he went into furious battle against 4500 Spanish troops. In spite of their obvious numerical disadvantage, the English were at first successful in driving the enemy back. But on the third charge, as he turned to retreat, Sidney was struck just above the left knee by a musketball. The bullet glanced upward, pulverizing his entire thighbone. After

[6]*The Life of Sir Philip Sidney*, p. 336.

two weeks he was thought out of danger, but then the wound grew worse, and he died a few days later, just a month before his thirty-second birthday.

AN APOLOGY FOR POETRY

Sidney's *Apology* gives a local habitation and a name to that airy nothingness, the "spirit" of English Renaissance literature. It is therefore not surprising that it has been, and will remain, an important point of departure for students of the age of Spenser, Shakespeare, Donne, and Milton. In the broadest terms its publication in 1595 marks the advent of neo-classicism in England. The notes to this edition should illustrate that the main lines of Sidney's esthetic run through the best of what was thought and said in his own time, but take their ultimate source in the eloquence of antiquity. The doctrine of imitation, the decision to rank poetry with the other arts and sciences, and an essentially philosophical approach to literature are Aristotle's most important legacies to the *Apology*. The notion that poetry sets forth veiled truths or allegories was not an idea that Plato would have agreed with, but it was, as Spenser's poetry well illustrates, a staple of Renaissance Platonizing. Sidney erected his treatise on the foundation of the classical oration, a literary form standardized for posterity in the prescriptions of Cicero and Quintilian.[7] Several other figures, notably Horace, Plutarch, and Seneca, fill out the main contours of this important classical background.

In the nearer foreground we can discern the depressing state of English poetry and poetic theory in the period that preceded the composition of the *Apology*. Since Chaucer there had been no English poet to compare with the masters of French and Italian poetry. The partial glory of Wyatt and Surrey was decades away, and the hiatus between was hardly prepossessing. Sackville's "Induction" had been a bright moment, and *Gor-*

[7]See Kenneth Orne Myrick, *Sir Philip Sidney as a Literary Craftsman* (1935), ch. 2.

boduc was technically commendable and had a certain style, but we must admit, with Sidney, that there had been many lean years since the beginning of Elizabeth's reign in 1558. True, there was good reason to praise *The Shepherd's Calendar* (1579), and word was out that Spenser was at work on a major heroic poem; but *The Faerie Queene*, along with most of the memorable Elizabethan poetry, was first published in the years following Sidney's death. Indeed, the tremendous flowering of English literature during the 1590s was in no small measure a response to Sidney's example.

The critical scene was only slightly more distinguished. In his *The Governor* (1531) Sir Thomas Elyot had placed poetry high among the subjects that mold a courtier and reaffirmed the Socratic equation of knowledge with virtue, a formula everywhere evident in the *Apology*. *The Schoolmaster* (1570) of Roger Ascham continued in the tradition of Elyot, but like its predecessor it offered no detailed and systematic critical theory. For this Sidney had to go abroad, to continental writers such as Scaliger and Minturno. In fact, of the literary disquisitions written in the years just prior to the *Apology*, perhaps the most influential was emphatically negative. In 1579 Stephen Gosson, a sometime poet and playwright turned social reformer, published *The School of Abuse*, a puritanical attack upon poets and players, dedicated to Sidney.[8] It has often been argued that this petulant little book provoked Sidney to take up his pen in defense of poetry, but the case is not a very strong one. Gosson spills most of his venom on the disreputable state of the contemporary stage, and in this position Sidney was more or less his ally. The charge that poems "slip downe into the hart, and with gunshotte of affection gaule the minde"[9] was not a new one, and not one that Sidney replies to directly. In fact, Gosson was

---

[8]Gosson subtitled his treatise "a plesaunt invective against Poets, Pipers, Plaiers, Jesters and such like Caterpillers of a Commonwealth." His most notable predecessor in the attack on poets was John Northbrooke, whose *Treatise against Dicing, Dancing, Plays, and Interludes* appeared in about 1577.

[9]*School*, p. 32.

small game. His sting may have caused the lion to roll over in his sleep, but only the likes of Plato could make him wake up and roar.

Sidney was not a "homely and familiar poet" addressing himself to the purely literary sensibilities of his fellow artists. The eclecticism of the *Apology* is a reflection of its author's deep submergence in the traditions of European culture. This broad intellectual base is an expression of Sidney's firmest conviction, that poetry, as the teacher *par excellence* of knowledge and virtue, is the monarch of the arts and sciences. In his division of the standard academic disciplines Sidney distinguishes between those that lead to a knowledge of things—such as astronomy, medicine, and law—and those that illuminate and instruct man about himself, and thus guide the student to the supreme goal of all learning, a life of active virtue. In this latter, "moral" category there are three major subdivisions—history, philosophy, poetry—and from the very outset it is Sidney's assurance that poetry is the most successful of the three in achieving the ethical objectives of knowledge.

This assurance, however, is not simply a dogmatic assertion in the *Apology*, but follows quite logically from what amounts to a scientific theory of communication. And this theory proceeds from two important premises. First, following Aristotle, Sidney assumes that the most useful knowledge involves universal or general ideas about vices and virtues, and not particular examples of this man's gluttony and that man's courage. In other words, true knowledge is abstract. Second, he takes the position that moral abstractions are most effective in moving us to virtue not when they are presented in verbal definitions, but when they are made graphically visible to our mind's eye. The first assumption makes it possible to exclude history from the competition, for the historian (according to Sidney) must concern himself with specific events and actual persons, and is therefore barred from the consideration of the abstract and general. The philosopher, on the other hand, concerned as he is with the knowledge of universals, fulfills the first requirement. But he falters on the second. Moral philosophy, for Sidney, is confined to the "wordish description," to the definition of ethical abstractions in words. Accordingly, while it may teach us what vices and virtues are, philosophy cannot move us with vivid pictures to put knowledge to active use.

Poetry succeeds where history and philosophy fail because it meets both of Sidney's pedagogical demands. It is superior to history because it deals with the general rather than the specific. Governed only by the laws of probability, the poet abandons historical fact and creates a world of more universal, and therefore more nearly perfect, ethical dimensions. The victory over philosophy is less decisive because the philosopher, unlike the historian, is similar to the poet in his preoccupation with moral abstractions. But the poet takes the laurel because he renders the precepts of "wordish" philosophy delightful by presenting them in a pictorial form. The fact that poetry can make ideas visible to the mind is the final key to its preeminence, for it guarantees that knowledge (*gnosis*) will manifest itself in virtuous action (*praxis*). We are constantly reminded that the poet creates something to be seen ("notable images of virtues, vices, or what else") simply because this quality is crucial to Sidney's theoretical explanation of his craft.

His logic notwithstanding, however, Sidney's definition of poetry as a "speaking picture" is extremely vague, and we may wonder what it is precisely that we are intended to see in a poem. By the word "speaking" he means that poets necessarily create in a verbal medium. This is clear enough. But the word "picture" is not so easily explained. It could mean that poetry is a kind of representational painting in words, an art of language in which there is a premium on vivid, picturesque descriptions of the phenomena of external nature. But such an interpretation goes sharply against the grain of the *Apology*, where moral abstractions, and not specific objects, are the poet-teacher's primary subject. Rather, as previously suggested, it is much more likely that by "picture" Sidney means an abstraction, a concept made visible to the reader's mind. "Picture" in this sense helps to explain the argument that poets, by coupling "the general notion with the particular example," produce "an image of that whereof the philosopher bestoweth but a wordish description." To put it another way, the poet allows his reader to see a moral universal in action by submerging it in a specific character. The best poet is like "the more excellent" kind of painter, who "painteth not Lucretia whom he never saw, but painteth the outward beauty of such a virtue." A good poem about Lucretia, according to such standards, would leave us with a clear picture of the virtue of constancy. By "speaking picture," then, Sidney means the poetic fusion of moral abstractions with actual characters. And if he is successful in this activity the poet sets "all virtues, vices, and passions so in their own natural seats laid to the view that we seem not to hear of them, but clearly to see through them."

It remains to consider how the poet constructs his "speaking picture," and how, when confronted with the completed artifact, the reader is expected to grasp its meaning. Sidney, it must be obvious, would have been dumbfounded with theories of poetry which gravitate toward subjectivism. Observing the rule that poets must "know what they do, and how they do," he finds his contemporaries devoid of "poetical sinews." The reduction of their poems to prose illustrates "that one verse did but beget another, without ordering at the first what should be at the last." As therapy for such spinelessness he grounds his theory of composition in the "*Idea* or fore-conceit of the work, and not in the work itself." The "*Idea* or fore-conceit" of a poem is its conceptual structure, and for Sidney it is imperative that the poet have this logical plan clearly visualized before he puts pen to paper. In composing a piece about Lucretia, for example, the writer's first task is to organize his ideas about constancy. This done, he is ready to put words on his thought. The result should be a verbal description of a particular woman, Lucretia, suspended on the scaffolding of a clearly preconceived moral abstraction—in short, a "speaking picture" of constancy.

In our reading of the completed poem Sidney expects that we

will exactly reverse the poet's procedure. An adept reader, as he puts it, will "use the narration" of the poem "as an imaginative ground-plot of a profitable invention." By "ground-plot" Sidney means a map or diagram, an abstract picture, and the term refers to the poet's original "fore-conceit" as it appears to the reader beneath the verbal veneer of the "speaking picture." Given this initial glimpse into the conceptual structure of the poem, we are meant to use it as the basis of our own "invention" (from Latin *invenire*, "to find" or "to come upon") or reconstruction of the full-scale "fore-conceit" as seen in the poet's mind. In the poem about Lucretia, for example, we should be able to look through the concrete details on the surface to the general *"Idea"* of constancy upon which they were originally modeled. At our labor's end we can expect to find ourselves just where the poet began, not with words, but with a moral universal squarely before our mind's eye.

Although *An Apology for Poetry* is very often read in isolation, its full implications will be most clear to those who use it as a prologue to the rest of the Sidney canon. We will do well, too, to remember that by "poetry" our author means all creative writing, and not simply verse. In fact, of all of Sidney's works, the prose in the revised *Arcadia* most fully exemplifies the doctrines set forth in the *Apology*. Here, as Fulke Greville observes, it was Sidney's objective to sketch "exact pictures, of every posture in the minde."[10] Accordingly, it is to this his longest, and perhaps least read, book that we should finally turn to see what he really meant.

Forrest G. Robinson
Cambridge, Massachusetts
June 1970

---

[10]*Life of Sir Philip Sidney*, p. 16.

Note on the Text

In 1595, almost ten years after Sidney's death, *An Apology for Poetry* was published in two different editions, with two different titles. For this edition I have selected the version published by Henry Olney, entitled *An Apology for Poetry*, as the basic text. Between Olney's text and its rival, *The Defense of Poesy*, published by William Ponsonby, there are numerous minor variations. When such variants improve the sense I have incorporated them into the text and added a note pointing out the addition. And when they offer interesting alternatives I have included them in the notes.

Thanks to a suggestion from Ian Watt, I have also collated the recently discovered Norwich MS, and again the substantial variants have either been incorporated into the text or mentioned in the notes. This very interesting, easily legible manuscript was uncovered a few years ago in England by an American scholar, Miss Mary Mahl. Miss Mahl very generously sent me a copy of her discovery and made several useful suggestions concerning the preparation of the text. I am especially grateful for her friendly help.

Spelling, punctuation, and such archaic forms as the long *s* have been modernized in the text. Quoted material in the notes retains the original spelling, though the peculiarities of Elizabethan typography have been adjusted to modern standards.

Finally, I would like to offer my thanks to Miss Carolyn Jakeman and the staff at the Houghton Library reading room for many small favors; to Walter Kaiser for suggesting the project in the first place; to Herschel Baker for his guidance and example; to Bruce Stovel and Charles Pierce for friendly corrections; to Miss Nancy Sullivan for her expert typing; to Mrs. Harold M. Gordon for the index; and to my wife for her enduring patience.

F. G. R.

Abbreviations in Notes and Introduction

ARTE: George Puttenham, *The Arte of English Poesie*, ed. G. D. Willcock and A. Walker (1936).

COOK: Sir Philip Sidney, *The Defense of Poesy*, ed. Albert S. Cook (1890).

DANIEL: Samuel Daniel, *Poems and A Defence of Ryme*, ed. Arthur Colby Sprague (1930).

GILBERT: *Literary Criticism: Plato to Dryden*, ed. Allen H. Gilbert (1940).

THE GOVERNOR: Sir Thomas Elyot, *The Governor*, Everyman ed. (1907).

NORWICH: The Norwich Manuscript of *An Apology for Poetry*.

OLNEY: Olney's text of the *Apology* (1595).

ORATIO: John Rainolds, *Oratio in Laudem Artis Poeticae*, ed. William Ringler, trans. Walter Allen, Jr. (1940).

POEMS: *The Poems of Sir Philip Sidney*, ed. William A. Ringler, Jr. (1965).

PONSONBY: Ponsonby's text of the *Apology* (1595).

SCHOOL: Stephen Gosson, *The School of Abuse*, ed. Edward Arber (1868).

SHEPHERD: Sir Philip Sidney, *An Apology for Poetry*, ed. Geoffrey Shepherd (1965).

SMITH: *Elizabethan Critical Essays,* ed. G. Gregory Smith, 2 vols. (1961).

WEINBERG: Bernard Weinberg, *A History of Literary Criticism in the Italian Renaissance, 2 vols.* (1961).

WORKS: *The Complete Works of Sir Philip Sidney,* ed. Albert Feuillerat, 4 vols. (1912–1926).

An Apology
for Poetry

An Apology for Poetry

When the right virtuous Edward Wotton[1] and I were at the Emperor's Court together, we gave ourselves to learn horsemanship of John Pietro Pugliano, one that with great commendation had the place of an esquire[2] in his stable. And he, according to the fertileness of the Italian wit, did not only afford us the demonstration of his practice, but sought to enrich our minds with the contemplations therein, which he thought most precious. But with none I remember mine ears were at any time more loaden, than when (either angered with slow payment, or moved with our learner-like admiration) he exercised his speech in the praise of his faculty. He said soldiers were the noblest estate of mankind, and horsemen the noblest of soldiers. He said they were the masters of war and ornaments of peace, speedy goers and strong abiders, triumphers both in camps and courts. Nay, to so unbelieved a point he proceeded, as that no earthly thing bred such wonder to a prince as to be a good horseman.[3]

---

[1]Edward Wotton (1548–1626), first Baron Wotton, was an English courtier and statesman. During his continental travels Sidney spent the winter of 1574–75 at the Imperial Court of Maximilian II in Vienna. In company with his mentor, Hubert Languet, Sidney engaged in a warm friendship with Wotton. At the end of May 1575, Wotton joined Sidney in Antwerp for the return voyage to England. A decade later Wotton was mentioned in Sidney's will and served as a pallbearer in the poet's funeral procession.

[2]An esquire, or equerry, was an officer in charge of the horses and stables of a noble personage.

[3]His irony notwithstanding, Sidney probably pursued both the theory ("contemplations") and practice of horsemanship with some seriousness.

Skill of government was but a *pedanteria*[4] in comparison. Then
would he add certain praises by telling what a peerless beast a
horse was; the only serviceable courtier without flattery, the
beast of most beauty, faithfulness, courage, and such more, that
if I had not been a piece of a logician[5] before I came to him, I
think he would have persuaded me to have wished myself a

In a letter to his brother Robert, dated October 1580, he suggested a training schedule very similar to the one he and Wotton followed with Pugliano.
"At horsemanshipp when yow exercise it reade Grison Claudio, and a
booke that is called *La gloria del cavallo*, withall, that yow may joyne the
through contemplation of it with the exercise, and so shall yow profite more
in a moneth then others in a yeare, and marke the bitting, sadling, and
curing of horses" (*Works*, III, 133). Cf. Dorus' masterful horsemanship
in *Arcadia* (*Works*, I, 178–79).

[4] Italian for pedantry.

[5] Sidney's interest in logic was probably stimulated by his contact with
Peter Ramus, a French dialectician, whose death in the Massacre of St.
Bartholomew brought him great popularity with English Calvinists. (Mac-
Ilmaine entitled his translation of 1574 *The Logike of the Most Excellent
Philosopher P. Ramus, Martyr*.) Sidney met Ramus in Paris in 1572, and
was undoubtedly dismayed at the bloodbath that occurred during his sojourn (see Introduction). Four years later Theophilus Banosius, whom
Sidney met in Vienna in 1574, published the posthumous *Petri Rami
Commentarium de Religione Christiana Libri Quatuor* (*The Commentary
of Peter Ramus on the Christian Religion in Four Books*), and dedicated
it to Sidney with the assurance that the young Englishman had loved Ramus
when he was alive, and esteemed his memory now that he was dead. During the 1570s Sidney's friend Gabriel Harvey was preaching the Ramist
gospel at Cambridge, primarily in his two orations, *Rhetor* and *Ciceronianus*.
In 1584 William Temple dedicated his edition of Ramus' *Dialectic* to
Sidney, and the poet responded with a letter of generous approval (*Works*,
III, 145). A few years before Temple's edition, at about the time of the
composition of the *Apology*, Abraham Fraunce was at work on the *Sheap-
heardes Logike*, which was subsequently dedicated to Sidney's close friend
Edward Dyer. The manuscript of this unpublished treatise is accompanied
by two shorter works (also by Fraunce): *Of the nature and use of Logike*,
and *A bryef and general comparison of Ramus his Logike wth that of Aristotle, to ye ryghte worshypful his very good Mr and Patron P: Sydney*
(British Museum Add. MS 34, 361). In the more familiar *Lawiers Logike*
(1588), Fraunce remarks that the earlier tracts were written when he "first
came in presence of that right noble and most renowmed knight sir Philip
Sydney." Fraunce's *Arcadian Rhetorike*, also published in 1588, is a clear
redaction of Ramist rhetorical principles, and is copiously illustrated with
quotations from Sidney's poetry.

horse. But thus much at least with his no few words he drave into me, that self-love is better than any gilding to make that seem gorgeous wherein ourselves are parties. Wherein, if Pugliano his strong affection and weak arguments will not satisfy you, I will give you a nearer example of myself, who (I know not by what mischance), in these my not old years and idlest times, having slipped into the title of a poet,[6] am provoked to say something unto you in the defence of that my unelected vocation, which if I handle with more good will than good reasons, bear with me, sith the scholar is to be pardoned that followeth the steps of his master.[7] And yet I must say that, as I have just cause to make a pitiful defence of poor poetry,[8] which from almost the highest estimation of learning is fallen to be the laughing-stock of children, so have I need to bring some more available[9] proofs, sith the former is by no man barred of his deserved credit, the silly[10] latter hath had even the names of philosophers used to the defacing of it, with great danger of civil war among the Muses.

And first, truly, to all them that, professing learning, inveigh against poetry, may justly be objected that they go very near to ungratefulness to seek to deface that which, in the noblest nations and languages that are known, hath been the first light-giver to ignorance, and first nurse, whose milk by little and little enabled them to feed afterwards of tougher knowledges.[11] And

[6]Sidney is probably referring to the original *Arcadia*, which he completed during the year or so that preceded the composition of the *Apology*.

[7]The irony is transparent enough. While sharing "good will," Sidney has no doubt that the logic of his discourse (his "reasons") will far exceed that of his "master" (Pugliano).

[8]It has been argued that Sidney had Stephen Gosson in mind when he wrote this passage, but the lament for "poor poetry" was commonplace among humanists. On Gosson, see Introduction.

[9]Capable of producing a desired result.

[10]Here used with an affectionate rather than pejorative connotation.

[11]The notion that poets were the first philosophers and the founders of learning had great currency during the Renaissance, though the idea was also common in antiquity. Boccaccio, for example, extrapolating from Aristotle, argues that the earliest Greek poets were also theologians (*The Life of Dante*, Gilbert, p. 211). Sidney may have been following the lead

will they now play the hedgehog that, being received into the den, drave out his host? Or rather the vipers, that with their birth kill their parents? Let learned Greece, in any of her manifold sciences, be able to show me one book before Musaeus,[12] Homer, and Hesiod,[13] all three nothing else but poets. Nay, let any history be brought that can say any writers were there before them, if they were not men of the same skill as Orpheus,[14] Linus,[15] and some other are named, who, having been the first of that country that made pens deliverers of their knowledge to their posterity, may justly challenge to be called their fathers in learning: for not only in time they had this priority (although in itself antiquity be venerable), but went before them, as causes to draw with their charming sweetness the wild untamed wits to an admiration of knowledge. So as Amphion[16] was said to

---

of Sir Thomas Elyot, who wrote (*The Governor*, p. 36): "I feare me to be longe from noble Homere: from whom as from a fountaine proceded all eloquence and lernyng." See also Puttenham (*Arte*, pp. 6 ff.).

[12]Musaeus, a mythical singer of antiquity, was often associated with Orpheus. Plato (*Republic*, II, 364) speaks of Musaeus and Orpheus as the descendants of the Muses and the Moon. Julius Scaliger, in his *Poetices* (I, 2), ranks Musaeus with Orpheus and Linus as poets of the second period of poetry, singers of religion and mysteries.

[13]Hesiod, a poet of Greece, is thought to have lived during the eighth century B.C. His *Theogony* is the first example of religious writing in Greek. He is also well known for *Works and Days*.

[14]Orpheus is perhaps best known for his unsuccessful attempt to rescue Eurydice from the underworld. In classical times he was thought to have founded Orphism, a religion of Dionysian mysteries. Horace (*Ars Poetica*, 390 ff.) mentions Orpheus as a poet and visionary, an advocate of civilized living and a tamer of wild beasts. See n. 12, above.

[15]Linus is the subject of a variety of contradictory accounts. By some he was considered the son of Amphimarus and Urania, slain by Apollo for the assertion that his singing was the equal of the god's, but other legends held that he was Heracles' music teacher. See n. 12, above.

[16]Amphion was the son of Zeus and Antiope. The association of Amphion and Orpheus in this passage suggests that Sidney's source was Horace (*Ars Poetica*, 390 ff.), who relates that the two singers were able to tame beasts and control inanimate objects through the magic of their music. (See n. 12, above.) Scaliger (*Poetices*, I, 2), probably following Horace, remarks that Amphion and Orpheus were religious poets with divine powers over the inanimate.

move stones with his poetry to build Thebes, and Orpheus to be listened to by beasts, indeed stony and beastly people, so among the Romans were Livius Andronicus[17] and Ennius.[18] So in the Italian language, the first that made it aspire to be a treasure-house of science were the poets Dante,[19] Boccaccio,[20] and Petrarch.[21] So in our English were Gower[22] and Chaucer, after whom, encouraged and delighted with their excellent fore-going, others have followed to beautify our mother tongue, as well in the same kind as in other arts.

This did so notably show itself, that the philosophers of Greece durst not a long time appear to the world but under the masks of poets. So Thales,[23] Empedocles,[24] and Parmenides[25]

---

[17]Livius Andronicus, a Latin poet of the third century B.C., was the composer of the first Latin comedy and the first Latin tragedy.

[18]Ennius, the so-called "father of Roman poetry," lived during the third and second centuries B.C. His only extant works are fragmentary. Horace (*Ars Poetica*, 259–62) criticizes him for slipshod workmanship.

[19]Dante (1265–1321) is most famous for his vernacular poetry, *The New Life* and *The Divine Comedy*. Sidney's reference to "science," however, suggests that he was thinking of two lesser known Latin treatises, *De Vulgari Eloquentia*, on Romance philology, and *De Monarchia*, concerned with the relations of church and state.

[20]Boccaccio (1313–1375) is best known for his collection of tales, *The Decameron*, which had considerable influence on Chaucer. Several of the tales from *The Decameron* appear in William Painter's *Palace of Pleasure*, first published in 1566.

[21]Petrarch (1304–1374), Italian poet and humanist, was an early advocate of the reconciliation of classical learning and Christian faith. Though esteemed for his scholarship, Petrarch is most often remembered for the tradition of love poetry which bears his name.

[22]Gower (ca. 1330–1408), "moral Gower," as Chaucer called him, was a prolific poet in French and Latin, though mentioned here for his English poem, *Confessio Amantis*.

[23]Thales of Miletus, accounted one of the Seven Sages, flourished during the sixth century B.C. His cosmology centered around the doctrine that water is the first principle of all things, the substratum from which all things are created, and into which they will ultimately pass away.

[24]Empedocles (fl. ca. 450 B.C.) of Acragas was famed as a poet, philosopher, orator, and doctor. Fragments of his writings have survived.

[25]Parmenides (fl. 475 B.C.) of Elea is best remembered for his trenchant commentary in Plato's dialogue, *Parmenides*. His hexameter philosophical

sang their natural philosophy in verses; so did Pythagoras[26] and
Phocylides[27] their moral counsels; so did Tyrtaeus[28] in war matters and Solon[29] in matters of policy: or rather, they being
poets, did exercise their delightful vein in those points of highest knowledge which before them lay hid to the world. For that
wise Solon was directly a poet, it is manifest, having written in
verse the notable fable of the Atlantic Island, which was continued by Plato.[30]

And truly, even Plato, whosoever well considereth shall find
that in the body of his work, though the inside and strength
were philosophy, the skin as it were and beauty depended most
of poetry,[31] for all standeth upon dialogues, wherein he feigneth
many honest burgesses of Athens to speak of such matters, that
if they had been set on the rack they would never have con-
fessed them; besides his poetical describing the circumstances of
their meetings, as the well ordering of a banquet, the delicacy
of a walk, with interlacing mere tales, as Gyges'[32] ring, and

---

poem, which sets forth the famous doctrine of the One, has survived in
large fragments.

[26]Pythagoras (fl. 532 B.C.) discovered the intervals of the musical scale,
and then proceeded to construe the entire universe in terms of numbers.
He founded a society in Croton which was devoted in part to religious
mysteries and in part to science.

[27]Phocylides (fl. 544 B.C.) of Miletus was an elegiac and hexameter poet.
Scaliger (*Poetices*, I, 2) includes him among the "moral" poets.

[28]Tyrtaeus (fl. 670 B.C.), an elegiac poet and military officer, was famous
for his war songs which (as Lodge puts it) "could incite men to the defence of theyr countrye" (*Defence of Poetry*, Smith, I, 75).

[29]Solon (fl. 600 B.C.) was an Athenian statesman and poet.

[30]For the story of the lost continent of Atlantis see Plato's *Timaeus*.

[31]The notion that Plato was a poet was a commonplace among Renaissance humanists, and had some currency even in classical antiquity. For a
precedent in England, see John Rainolds, *Oratio*, p. 41. For a fuller discussion, see Shepherd, pp. 148–49.

[32]Gyges (fl. 675 B.C.) was for nearly thirty years the king of Lydia. The
story of his magic ring appears in Plato's *Republic*, II, 359. The power of
the ring enabled Gyges to make himself invisible and thus take complete
command of a kingdom. The same story appears in Cicero's *De Officiis*,
III, ix, 38–39.

others, which who knoweth not to be flowers of poetry did
never walk into Apollo's garden.[33]

And even historiographers (although their lips sound of
things done, and verity be written in their foreheads) have been
glad to borrow both fashion and perchance weight of poets. So
Herodotus entitled his *History* by the name of the nine Muses,[34]
and both he and all the rest that followed him either stole or
usurped of poetry their passionate describing of passions, the
many particularities of battles, which no man could affirm; or, if
that be denied me, long orations put in the mouths of great
kings and captains, which it is certain they never pronounced.
So that truly, neither philosopher nor historiographer could at
the first have entered into the gates of popular judgments if
they had not taken a great passport of poetry, which, in all nations at this day where learning flourisheth not, is plain to be
seen; in all which they have some feeling of poetry.

In Turkey, besides their law-giving divines, they have no other
writers but poets. In our neighbor country Ireland, where truly
learning goeth very bare, yet are their poets held in a devout
reverence.[35] Even among the most barbarous and simple Indians
where no writing is, yet have they their poets, who make and
sing songs which they call *areytos*,[36] both of their ancestors'
deeds and praises of their gods; a sufficient probability that, if
ever learning come among them, it must be by having their hard

[33]Have no sense of what it is that constitutes true poetry.

[34]Herodotus (ca. 480–ca. 425 B.C.), a Greek historian, was born at Hali-
carnassus. He is remembered as "the father of history" because of his
unprecedented precision and accuracy. His *History* is divided into nine
books, each named after one of the Muses, but it is thought that this division was made by Alexandrian editors.

[35]Apart from their famous bards, the Irish had little to recommend them
to Sidney. Like his father, who was the queen's viceroy in Ireland for many
years, Sidney viewed the Roman Catholic Irish as uncivilized barbarians.
It is probable that he visited Ireland in 1576.

[36]This was a ceremonial dance accompanied by songs, common among
the Indians in the Americas. Sidney's information was apparently derived
from Peter Martyr's *Decades*, which appeared in Richard Eden's *Hystorie
of the West Indies* (1555). See Cook, pp. 67–68.

dull wits softened and sharpened with the sweet delights of poetry. For until they find a pleasure in the exercises of the mind, great promises of much knowledge will little persuade them that know not the fruits of knowledge. In Wales, the true remnant of the ancient Britons,[37] as there are good authorities to show the long time they had poets which they called *bards*, so through all the conquests of Romans, Saxons, Danes, and Normans, some of whom did seek to ruin all memory of learning from among them, yet do their poets even to this day last, so as it is not more notable in soon beginning than in long continuing.

But since the authors of most of our sciences were the Romans, and before them the Greeks, let us a little stand upon their authorities, but even so far as to see what names they have given unto this now scorned skill. Among the Romans a poet was called *vates*, which is as much as a diviner, foreseer, or prophet, as by his conjoined words *vaticinium* and *vaticinari* is manifest; so heavenly a title did that excellent people bestow upon this heart-ravishing knowledge. And so far were they carried into the admiration thereof, that they thought in the chanceable hitting upon any such verses great fore-tokens of their following fortunes were placed. Whereupon grew the word of *Sortes Virgilianae*,[38] when by sudden opening Virgil's book they lighted upon any verse of his making,[39] whereof the His-

[37]The popular notion that Brutus (the great-grandson of Aeneas) was the founder of the British race was still current in the sixteenth century. Geoffrey of Monmouth (ca. 1100–ca. 1155) initiated the legend in his Latin *History of the Kings of Britain*, claiming a secret book as his source. Geoffrey's fanciful historiography became a fertile authority for the medieval romance writers and was the source of Spenser's chronicle of British kings in *The Faerie Queene*. Hideous giants ruled the countryside

> Until that Brutus, anciently deriv'd
> From roiall stocke of old Assaracs line,
> Driven by fatall error here arriv'd,
> And them of their unjust possession depriv'd (*II, x, 9*).

The same story appears in Michael Drayton's *Poly-Olbion*, I, 312 ff.

[38]A kind of literary prophecy. A volume of Virgil is opened at random, and the first passage fallen upon is purported to foretell future events.

[39]Ponsonby: "verse of his, as it is reported by many, whereof . . ."

tories of the Emperors' Lives are full: as of Albinus, the governor of our island, who in his childhood met with this verse,

Arma amens capio nec sat rationis in armis,

and in his age performed it;[40] which, although it were a very vain and godless superstition, as also it was to think that spirits were commanded by such verses—whereupon this word charms, derived of *carmina,*[41] cometh—so yet serveth it to show the great reverence those wits were held in. And altogether not without ground, since both the oracles of Delphos[42] and Sibylla's[43] prophecies were wholly delivered in verses. For that same exquisite observing of number and measure in words, and that high flying liberty of conceit[44] proper to the poet, did seem to have some divine force in it.

And may not I presume a little further, to show the reasonableness of this word *vates*, and say that the holy David's Psalms are a divine poem?[45] If I do, I shall not do it without the testi-

[40]Albinus was an aggressive soldier who, after a period of distinguished military service, became the governor of Britain. Covetous of an emperor's power, and encouraged by prophetic signs in his youth, Albinus was proclaimed emperor by his troops, but failed in his march on Rome and was killed in battle in A.D. 197. Even as a boy Albinus revealed his warlike nature by repeating to his peers, "Madly I seized my arms, although there was little reason in arms" (*Aeneid*, II, 314). The story is related in the life of *Albinus Clodius*, V, 2, in *Scriptores Historiae Augustae.* Sidney's irony is at Albinus' expense, for there was clearly little reason in taking arms.

[41]Nominative plural of the Latin *carmen*, a song, poem, or incantation.

[42]Delphos, or Delphi, was in antiquity the location of the Delphic Oracle. The site was considered the center of the earth, marked by the sacred *omphalos*. The presiding deity was Apollo, at whose temple the woman Pythia delivered prophetic riddles. Sidney made use of the Oracle in the *Arcadia* (*Works*, IV, 2), complete with "furiously inspired" obscurities that turn out to be all too true.

[43]Originally a single prophetic female, the Sibyl was gradually pluralized into a number of local personages. The Sibylline prophecies, as described by Virgil (*Aeneid*, VI, 77 ff.), were ecstatic verse riddles like those delivered at Delphi. Thomas Lodge (*Defence of Poetry*, Smith, I, 71), in anticipation of Sidney, remarked that "all the answeares of the Oracles weare in verse." Cf. Horace, *Ars Poetica*, 400 ff.

[44]A concept.

[45]It was commonly agreed that David had been divinely inspired in his composition of the Psalms. Sidney himself translated the Psalter into a

mony of great learned men, both ancient and modern. But even
the name Psalms will speak for me, which being interpreted is
nothing but songs; then, that it is fully written in meter, as all
learned hebricians agree, although the rules be not yet fully
found; lastly and principally, his handling his prophecy, which
is merely poetical. For what else is the awaking his musical in-
struments, the often and free changing of persons, his notable
prosopopoeias,[46] when he maketh you, as it were, see God coming in His majesty, his telling of the beasts' joyfulness, and hills
leaping, but a heavenly poesy,[47] wherein almost he showeth
himself a passionate lover of that unspeakable and everlasting
beauty to be seen by the eyes of the mind, only cleared by
faith?[48] But truly, now having named him, I fear me I seem to
profane that holy name, applying it to poetry, which is among
us thrown down to so ridiculous an estimation. But they that
with quiet judgments will look a little deeper into it, shall find
the end and working of it such, as being rightly applied, deserveth not to be scourged out of the Church of God.

But now let us see how the Greeks named it and how they
deemed of it. The Greeks called him a poet, which name hath,
as the most excellent, gone through other languages. It cometh
of this word *poiein*, which is, to make, wherein I know not
whether by luck or wisdom we Englishmen have met with the
Greeks in calling him a maker:[49] which name, how high and

variety of English meters, though his enterprise was not without consider-
able precedent. See Ringler's notes (*Poems*, pp. 500 ff.), and Hallett Smith,
"English Metrical Psalms in the Sixteenth Century and Their Literary
Significance," *Huntington Library Quarterly*, IX (1946), 249–71.

[46]This is a Greek term, perhaps best rendered "personification," in which
an inanimate object or abstraction is endowed with human attributes.

[47]Sidney is generally careful to distinguish between "poetry," the finished
product of the poet's art, and "poesy," the craft or technique of writing. A
somewhat similar distinction appears in Scaliger's *Poetices* (I, 2).

[48]The notion that faith serves to clarify inner vision was a commonplace
in Christian thought. For example, see John Colet's commentary on St.
Paul's Epistle to the Romans, trans. J. H. Lupton (London, 1873), p. 46.

[49]In nominating the poet "a maker," Sidney was probably following
Scaliger (*Poetices*, I, 1). Indeed, a goodly portion of the argument in the
following paragraphs is taken from Scaliger. See Shepherd, pp. 155–56.

incomparable a title it is, I had rather were known by marking the scope of other sciences than by my partial allegation.

There is no art delivered to mankind that hath not the works of nature for his principal object, without which they could not consist, and on which they so depend, as they become actors and players, as it were, of what nature will have set forth. So doth the astronomer look upon the stars, and by that he seeth, setteth down what order nature hath taken therein. So do the geometrician and arithmetician in their diverse sorts of quantities. So doth the musician in times tell you which by nature agree, which not. The natural philosopher thereon hath his name, and the moral philosopher standeth upon the natural virtues, vices, and passions of man;[50] and follow nature (saith he) therein, and thou shalt not err.[51] The lawyer saith what men have determined; the historian what men have done. The grammarian speaketh only of the rules of speech, and the rhetorician and logician, considering what in nature will soonest prove and persuade, thereon give artificial[52] rules, which still are compassed within the circle of a question, according to the proposed matter.[53] The physician weigheth the nature of a man's body,

[50]In a letter to his brother Robert (*Works*, III, 131), Sidney defines the moral philosopher as one who "setts forth vertues or vices and the natures of Passions."

[51]A very common Stoic prescription. Cf. Cicero, *De Officiis*, I, xxviii, 97–98.

[52]Part of an established discipline or art. The usage here bears none of the pejorative connotations ("fictitious," "unnatural") current today.

[53]The rhetorician and logician, unlike the poet, must limit themselves to the terms and issues of the topic under consideration ("the circle of a question"). Sidney's confusion of logic and rhetoric, whether or not intended, is probably a result of his acquaintance with Ramism. Traditionally, logic was the art of making true statements in syllogisms, while rhetoric had persuasion rather than demonstration as its end, and employed enthymemes (arguments based on probable premises) rather than full-scale syllogisms. Classical rhetoric was divided into five parts: invention, disposition, elocution, memory, and pronunciation. In the Ramist system, however, rhetoric was limited to elocution and pronunciation, memory was dropped altogether, and invention and disposition were placed in the domain of logic. But the result of this division between logic and rhetoric was more nominal than real, for Ramist rhetoric was contingent upon the

and the nature of things helpful or hurtful unto it. And the metaphysic, though it be in the second and abstract notions, and therefore be counted supernatural, yet doth he indeed build upon the depth of nature.[54] Only the poet, disdaining to be tied to any such subjection, lifted up with the vigor of his own invention, doth grow in effect another nature, in making things either better than nature bringeth forth, or quite anew, forms such as never were in nature, as the Heroes, Demigods, Cyclops, Chimeras, Furies, and such like; so as he goeth hand in hand with nature, not enclosed within the narrow warrant of her gifts, but freely ranging only within the zodiac of his own wit.[55]

---

effective use of logic. Before statements of any kind could be made it was necessary, in theory at least, to invent and dispose the materials that the statements would articulate. Where classical rhetoric could be distinguished from logic, Ramist rhetoric was useless in the absence of logic. As a result it was almost inevitable that the two would overlap, as they do here in Sidney's discourse.

[54]The metaphysician ("metaphysic") is not concerned with specific sense impressions (first notions), but with universals which have been abstracted from sensory experience. Sidney's psychology is Aristotelian at this point, for his assurance that "second and abstract notions" are derived from "the depth of nature" implies that the forms conceived in the mind are immanent in the natural world.

[55]Sidney's argument here is in many ways similar to Shakespeare's in *A Midsummer Night's Dream* (V, i, 12–17):

> The poet's eye, in a fine frenzy rolling,
> Doth glance from heaven to earth, from earth to heaven;
> And as imagination bodies forth
> The forms of things unknown, the poet's pen
> Turns them to shapes, and gives to airy nothing
> A local habitation and a name.

The immediate source of the passage is almost certainly Scaliger, *Poetices*, I, 1. (See Shepherd, pp. 155–56, for a review of Scaliger's main points.) Sidney's position, though striking at first glance, is a commonplace in the history of ideas. Classical psychology held that the human intellect, through the faculty of imagination, could construct new forms from the conceptual materials already abstracted from sensation. Concepts are by definition superior to the things "nature bringeth forth," for they are universals. But Sidney's new forms "such as never were in nature" are emphatically unnatural, for they result from the mind's activity upon itself, and not upon the external world. Since all thought begins with sensations and concepts derived from nature, the poet necessarily "goeth hand in hand with nature,"

Nature never set forth the earth in so rich tapestry as divers poets have done, neither with pleasant rivers, fruitful trees, sweet smelling flowers, nor whatsoever else may make the too much loved earth more lovely. Her world is brazen, the poets only deliver a golden.

But let those things alone and go to man, for whom as the other things are, so it seemeth in him her uttermost cunning is employed, and know whether she have brought forth so true a lover as Theagenes,[56] so constant a friend as Pylades,[57] so valiant a man as Orlando,[58] so right a prince as Xenophon's Cyrus,[59] so excellent a man every way as Virgil's Aeneas.[60] Neither let

---

but in exceeding the limits of his natural perceptions, he is free to range "within the zodiac of his own wit." In effect, then, the poet is not distinguished by his imaginative faculties, for these are common to all thinking men. But the discipline of poetry, because it allows for and even encourages the use of the imagination, is distinguished from the rest of the liberal arts.

Sidney's psychology in this sentence, as in the one preceding, is Aristotelian, but the idea was so common that a definite source is unlikely to be found. For a precedent, however, cf. Girolamo Fracastoro, *Naugerius, Sive de Poetica Dialogus*, trans. Ruth Kelso (Urbana, Illinois, 1924), p. 60.

[56]Theagenes was the hero of *Aethiopica* or *Theagenes and Chariclea*, a Greek prose romance by Heliodorus of Emesa (fl. fourth century A.D.). Theagenes falls in love with Chariclea and steals her away. After many adventures they arrive in Ethiopia where Chariclea is discovered to be the king's daughter. The story was very popular during the Renaissance, and may have been a model for *Arcadia*.

[57]Pylades was the proverbial friend and aid of Orestes. After the death of Agamemnon, Orestes was secretly transported to the court of Pylades' father, where the two young men became friends. Cf. *The Faerie Queene*, IV, x, 27.

[58]Orlando is the Italian form of Roland, a hero of the romances of Charlemagne. During the Renaissance, however, Orlando was the hero of several Italian heroic poems, most notably Ariosto's *Orlando Furioso* (1532). The poem was translated into English in 1591 by Sir John Harington.

[59]Cyrus, the subject of Xenophon's (ca. 430–ca. 350 B.C.) fanciful political treatise, *Cyropaedia*, was a soldier of vast conquests, and the founder of the Achaemenid Persian Empire. To Renaissance humanists, as to the Greeks, Cyrus became the model of the just and magnanimous ruler.

[60]Cf. "A Letter of the Authors" prefixed to *The Faerie Queene*. Spenser argues that Homer, "in the Persons of Agamemnon and Ulysses hath ensampled a good governour and a vertuous man," and that Virgil combined both virtues "in the person of Aeneas."

this be jestingly conceived, because the works of the one be
essential,[61] the other in imitation or fiction; for any understanding knoweth the skill of the artificer standeth in that *Idea*
or fore-conceit of the work, and not in the work itself. And that
the poet hath that *Idea* is manifest by delivering them forth in
such excellency as he hath imagined them. Which delivering
forth also is not wholly imaginative, as we are wont to say by
them that build castles in the air, but so far substantially it
worketh, not only to make a Cyrus, which had been but a particular excellency, as nature might have done, but to bestow a
Cyrus upon the world to make many Cyruses, if they will learn
aright why and how that maker made him.[62]

Poet

[61]Actual or real, as opposed to something "in imitation or fiction."

[62]"Idea" is defined in Thomas Cooper's *Thesaurus* (1565) as a "figure
conceived in Imagination, as it were a substance perpetuall, beyng as paterne
of all other sorte or kinde, as of one seale procedeth many printes so of one
Idea of man procede many thousandes of men." Sidney's "Idea," like Cooper's, is a mental object, a generic concept which comprehends an abundant
variety of particular objects in any class. If the poet can translate his general
"Idea" into the words of a poem, then he will have produced a moral example superior to the specific or particular objects of external nature. Like
Cooper's "Idea," the poet's Cyrus is not an example of "a particular excellency, as nature might have done," but a Cyrus who will illustrate all the
virtues of an ideal ruler. It is upon this distinction between the ideal and
the real that Spenser, perhaps following Sidney, compares Xenophon and
Plato ("A Letter of the Authors," prefixed to *The Faerie Queene*): "For
this cause is Xenophon preferred before Plato, for that the one, in the exquisite depth of his judgement, formed a Commune welth, such as it
should be; but the other in the person of Cyrus, and the Persians, fashioned
a government, such as might best be: So much more profitable and gratious
is doctrine by ensample, then by rule."

"Conceit," or concept, as Sidney understood the term, was a general topic
beneath which the specific details of that topic (one of the arts, for example) might be arranged and observed. This is clear from the ruminations of
Pyrocles, one of the princes in *Arcadia* (*Works*, IV, 203). Although he has
reached a "Confused Conceypte" of a particular plan, Pyrocles has "not
sett downe" in his "fancy the meeting with eache particularity that mighte
falle oute." This comprehension of the specific in the general was probably
in Sidney's thoughts when he drew his portrait of Evarchus in *Arcadia*
(*Works*, I, 187). Since Evarchus is an example of an ideal ruler, it is quite
probable that Xenophon's Cyrus, the pattern for "many Cyruses," was his
model. Evarchus "with his people made all but one politike bodie, whereof
himselfe was the head; even so cared for them, as he woulde for his owne

exemplar

Neither let it be deemed too saucy a comparison to balance the highest point of man's wit with the efficacy of nature, but rather give right honor to the heavenly Maker of that maker, who having made man to His own likeness, set him beyond and over all the works of that second nature, which in nothing he showeth so much as in poetry, when with the force of a divine breath he bringeth things forth far surpassing her doings,[63] with no small argument to the incredulous of that first accursed fall of Adam: sith our erected wit maketh us know what perfection is, and yet our infected will keepeth us from reaching unto it.[64] But these arguments will by few be understood, and by fewer granted.

---

limmes: never restrayning their liberty, without it stretched to licenciousness, nor pulling from them their goods, which they found were not imployed to the purchase of a greater good: but in all his actions shewing a delight to their welfare, broght that to passe, that while by force he tooke nothing, by their love he had all. In summe (peerlesse Princesse) I might as easily sette down the whole Arte of government, as to lay before your eyes the picture of his proceedings."

[63]The poet, like God, creates with general concepts, and not external particulars, as his models. This notion, though common enough among philosophers, was perhaps suggested to Sidney in *A Woorke concerning the trewnesse of the Christian Religion*, a treatise by the Frenchman Phillipe de Mornay, first published in 1581, which Sidney had begun to translate before he left for the Netherlands. Writing in a tradition that runs all the way back to Plato, de Mornay argues that God created the *Logos*, the second person of the trinity, "which some translate *Word* or *Speech*, and othersome *Reason*." "And," he adds, "we say that by the same Speech or word, God made al things." In the same way, man's reason results in the creation of words and statements. "There is in man a dubble Speech; the one in the mynd, which they call the inward Speech, which wee conceyve afore we utter it; and the other the sounding image thereof, which is uttered by our mouth and is termed the Speech of the Voyce." By virtue of his knowledge of general concepts, man has some access to the patterns according to which God created the world, the ideas (or first nature) which underlie the particulars of "all the works of that second nature." The poet, like the craftsman (as de Mornay puts it), "maketh his worke by the patterne which he had erst conceyved in his mynde, which patterne is his inward word: so God made the World and all that is therein, by that sayd Speech of his as by his inward skill or arte" (*Works*, III, 266–68).

[64]It is central to Sidney's conception of the poet's function that he not only teach, but that he move the reader to embrace that which has been taught.

Thus much (I hope) will be given me, that the Greeks with some probability of reason gave him the name above all names of learning.

Now let us go to a more ordinary opening of him, that the truth may be more palpable: and so I hope, though we get not so unmatched a praise as the etymology of his names will grant, yet his very description, which no man will deny, shall not justly be barred from a principal commendation.

Poesy therefore is an art of imitation, for so Aristotle termeth it in this word *mimesis*, that is to say, a representing, counterfeiting, or figuring forth—to speak metaphorically, a speaking picture—with this end, to teach and delight.[65] Of this have been three several kinds.[66]

The chief both in antiquity and excellency were they that did imitate the inconceivable excellencies of God. Such were David in his Psalms, Solomon in his Song of Songs, in his Ecclesiastes and Proverbs, Moses and Deborah in their Hymns, and the writer of Job; which, beside other, the learned Emanuel Tremellius and Franciscus Junius[67] do entitle the poetical part of the Scripture. Against these none will speak that hath the Holy Ghost in due holy reverence. In this kind, though in a full wrong

[65]"Imitation" is misleading in this context, for it can be understood to mean the exact duplication of external objects. This confusion is intensified by Sidney's allusion to the doctrine of *ut pictura poesis*, which suggests that poetry and painting are sister arts, alike in their rendering of natural things. By "speaking picture," however, Sidney means that a poem is a general or universal concept (a "picture" seen in the mind) presented through the medium of language ("speaking"). The poet imitates his own "Idea or foreconceit," not the brazen world of "second nature."

For further discussion see Rensselaer W. Lee, "*Ut Pictura Poesis*: The Humanistic Theory of Painting," *The Art Bulletin*, XXII (1940), 197–269 (republished in book form in 1967). There are numerous precedents for the "as painting, so poetry" doctrine, though Horace (*Ars Poetica*, 360 ff.) and Plutarch (*Moralia, How to Study Poetry*, 3) are the most important.

[66]Sidney is probably following Scaliger (*Poetices*, I, 2) in his division.

[67]Emanuel Tremellius (1510–1580), a Jew of Ferrara converted to Protestantism, and Franciscus Junius (1545–1602), a French Protestant, together produced a Latin version of the Bible.

divinity, were Orpheus,[68] Amphion,[69] Homer in his Hymns,[70] and many other, both Greeks and Romans. And this poesy must be used by whosoever will follow St. James[71] his counsel in singing psalms when they are merry, and I know is used with the fruit of comfort by some, when in sorrowful pangs of their death-bringing sins, they find the consolation of the never-leaving goodness.

The second kind is of them that deal with matters philosophical: either moral, as Tyrtaeus,[72] Phocylides,[73] and Cato;[74] or natural, as Lucretius,[75] and Virgil's *Georgics*;[76] or astronomical, as Manilius[77] and Pontanus;[78] or historical, as Lucan:[79] which who mislike, the fault is in their judgments quite out of taste, and not in the sweet food of sweetly uttered knowledge.

But because this second sort is wrapped within the fold of the proposed subject, and takes not the course of his own invention, whether they properly be poets or no let grammarians dis-

[68]See n. 14, above.

[69]See n. 16, above.

[70]The Homeric Hymns are of unknown authorship, and consist of preludes to epics and Greek legends. They were translated by George Chapman in the early seventeenth century.

[71]"Is any among you afflicted? let him pray. Is any merry? let him sing psalms" (James 5:13).

[72]See n. 28, above.

[73]See n. 27, above.

[74]Cato, the so-called Dionysius Cato (third century A.D.), was the author of the *Distichs*, a popular textbook and source of moral lore during the Renaissance. See Smith, I, 65.

[75]Lucretius (ca. 99–55 B.C.), a Roman poet, whose hexameter poem, *De Rerum Natura*, popularized the Epicurean philosophy of atomism.

[76]Virgil's *Georgics* is a didactic poem, in four books, on various aspects of agriculture.

[77]Manilius was a Roman poet who lived during the time of Augustus and Tiberius. His *Astronomica* is a didactic poem on astrology.

[78]Pontanus, the Latin name of Giovanni Pontano (1426–1503), whose poem on the stars, *Urania*, Sidney may have known. Both Minturno and Castelvetro link Manilius and Pontano as astrological poets (see Gilbert, pp. 287 and 307).

[79]Lucan (A.D. 39–65), a Roman poet, whose *Pharsalia* recounts the wars between Pompey and Caesar.

pute,[80] and go to the third, indeed right poets, of whom chiefly this question ariseth. Betwixt whom and these second is such a kind of difference as betwixt the meaner sort of painters (who counterfeit only such faces as are set before them), and the more excellent, who having no law but wit, bestow that in colors upon you which is fittest for the eye to see: as the constant though lamenting look of Lucretia[81] when she punished in herself another's fault. Wherein he painteth not Lucretia whom he never saw, but painteth the outward beauty of such a virtue. For these third be they which most properly do imitate to teach and delight, and to imitate borrow nothing of what is, hath been, or shall be, but range only reined with learned discretion into the divine consideration of what may be and should be.[82] These be they that, as the first and most noble sort, may justly be termed *vates*, so these are waited on in the excellentest languages and best understandings with the fore-described name of poets. For these indeed do merely make to imitate, and imitate both to delight and teach, and delight to move men to take that goodness in hand which without delight they would fly as from a stranger, and teach, to make them know that goodness whereunto they are moved: which being the noblest scope to which ever any learning was directed, yet want there not idle tongues to bark at them.[83]

[80]The "philosophical" poet, like the rhetorician and logician (see n. 53, above), is limited to the specific materials of the subject under discussion.

[81]In legend Lucretia was the wife of Tarquinius Collatinus, who vindicated her honor by committing suicide after having been raped by Sextus Tarquinius.

[82]The most important classical precedent for Sidney's argument occurs in Aristotle's *Poetics*, XXV, where the poet, like the portrait painter, is instructed to preserve the type, and yet make it more noble. Fracastoro echoes this position in *Naugerius* (trans. Kelso, p. 60), though he adds the qualification that painters "imitate the particular," while "the poet imitates not the particular but the simple idea clothed in its own beauties, which Aristotle calls the universal." Like Fracastoro, Sidney distinguishes between pictorial representations of individual external objects, and the conceptual image of the universal, pictures "of what may be and should be." See n. 63, above.

[83]Sidney concurs with the Horatian dictum that poetry should be both

These be subdivided into sundry more special denominations.
The most notable be the Heroic, Lyric, Tragic, Comic, Satiric,
Iambic, Elegiac, Pastoral, and certain others, some of these
being termed according to the matter they deal with, some by
the sorts of verses they liked best to write in. For indeed the
greatest part of poets have apparelled their poetical inventions
in that numbrous[84] kind of writing which is called verse; indeed
but apparelled, verse being but an ornament and no cause to
poetry, sith there have been many most excellent poets that
never versified, and now swarm many versifiers that need never
answer to the name of poets.[85] For Xenophon,[86] who did imitate so excellently as to give us *effigiem justi imperii,* the por-
traiture of a just empire, under the name of Cyrus (as Cicero
saith of him[87]), made therein an absolute heroical poem. So did
Heliodorus in his sugared invention of that picture of love in
Theagenes and Cariclea,[88] and yet both these writ in prose:
which I speak to show, that it is not rhyming and versing that
maketh a poet, no more than a long gown maketh an advocate,
who though he pleaded in armor should be an advocate and no
soldier. But it is that feigning notable images of virtues, vices,
or what else,[89] with that delightful teaching, which must be the
right describing note to know a poet by: although indeed the
senate of poets hath chosen verse as their fittest raiments, mean-

---

profitable and pleasurable (*Ars Poetica,* 333 ff.), but adds that it should
also "move" the reader. Knowledge, particularly for those of a Calvinistic
inclination, was considered an insufficient basis for moral action; for although "our erected wit maketh us know what perfection is . . . our infected will keepeth us from reaching unto it" (p. 17, above). For a more
detailed discussion, see n. 180, below.

[84]Adhering to certain meters.

[85]Sidney is clearly more concerned with the content of poetry than with
its form. His distinction is identical to Elyot's (*The Governor,* p. 56): "They
that make verses, expressynge therby none other lernynge but the craft of
versifyeng, be nat of auncient writers named poetes, but onely called versi-
fyers."

[86]See n. 59, above.

[87]See Cicero's *Epistles to His Brother Quintus,* I, viii, 23 ff.

[88]See n. 56, above.

[89]See n. 50, above.

ing, as in matter they passed all in all, so in manner to go beyond them, not speaking (table talk fashion, or like men in a
dream) words as they chanceably fall from the mouth, but
peizing[90] each syllable of each word by just proportion according
to the dignity of the subject.

Now therefore it shall not be amiss first to weigh this latter
sort of poetry by his works, and then by his parts, and if in
neither of these anatomies he be condemnable, I hope we shall
obtain a more favorable sentence. This purifying of wit, this
enriching of memory, enabling of judgment, and enlarging of
conceit, which commonly we call learning, under what name
soever it come forth, or to what immediate end soever it be directed, the final end is to lead and draw us to as high a perfection as our degenerate souls, made worse by their clayey lodgings,
can be capable of. This, according to the inclination of the man,
bred many formed impressions.[91] For some that thought this
felicity principally to be gotten by knowledge,[92] and no knowledge to be so high and heavenly as acquaintance with the stars,
gave themselves to astronomy; others, persuading themselves to
be demi-gods if they knew the causes of things,[93] became
natural and supernatural philosophers;[94] some an admirable delight drew to music; and some, the certainty of demonstration,
to the mathematics. But all, one and other, having this scope, to
know, and by knowledge to lift up the mind from the dungeon
of the body to the enjoying his own divine essence. But when
by the balance of experience it was found that the astronomer,
looking to the stars, might fall into a ditch,[95] that the inquiring

[90]Weighing.

[91]Each man, according to the disposition of his faculties, is drawn to one
or another of the arts and sciences.

[92]The Socratic equation of knowledge and virtue had great currency with
Renaissance humanists, though the doctrines of Luther and Calvin did
much to undermine this optimistic view of human reason. For a lucid summary of the classical tradition, see Herschel Baker, *The Dignity of Man*
(1947), chs. 2 and 3.

[93]Cf. Virgil, *Georgics*, II, 490–91.

[94]Metaphysicians. See n. 54, above.

[95]Although the story of the stumbling astronomer was a commonplace,
the classical original appears in Plato's *Theaetetus* (174), where Socrates

productive means to higher end

philosopher might be blind in himself, and the mathematician might draw forth a straight line with a crooked heart, then lo did proof, the overruler of opinions, make manifest that all these are but serving sciences,[96] which, as they have each a private end in themselves, so yet are they all directed to the highest end of the mistress knowledge, by the Greeks called *architectonike*, which stands (as I think) in the knowledge of a man's self, in the ethic and politic consideration, with the end of well doing and not of well knowing only:[97] even as the saddler's next end is to make a good saddle, but his farther end, to serve a nobler faculty, which is horsemanship; so the horseman's to soldiery, and the soldier not only to have the skill, but to perform the practice of a soldier. So that, the ending end of all earthly learning, being virtuous action, those skills that most serve to bring forth that have a most just title to be princes over all the rest.

Wherein if we can show the[98] poet's nobleness by setting him before his other competitors, among whom as principal challengers step forth the moral philosophers, whom, me thinketh, I see coming towards me with a sullen gravity, as though they

---

relates that Thales (see n. 23, above) tumbled into a well while gazing at the stars. Sidney uses the same story in *Astrophil and Stella*, XIX (*Poems*, p. 174).

[96]Like logic and rhetoric (see n. 53, above), the "serving sciences" have certain fixed boundaries.

[97]Following Aristotle (*Nicomachean Ethics*, I, 2), Sidney argues that the arts and sciences culminate in a master (*architectonike*) science which comprehends the knowledge of the ultimate human good. But where Aristotle designates politics as the supreme discipline, Sidney selects that self-knowledge which results in "well doing." This distinction, however, is somewhat misleading. The moral philosopher, as Sidney describes him to his brother Robert (*Works*, III, 131), prescribes guidelines for both personal and public activity: "either in the ethick part when he setts forth vertues or vices and the natures of Passions, or in the Politick when he doth (as often he doth) meddle sententiouslie with matters of Estate." Since both "the ethic and politic" considerations appear here in the *Apology*, it is probable that "well doing" is not merely a norm for the regulation of "vertues and vices," but shades off into "matters of Estate," or politics, as well.

[98]Ponsonby: "the poet is worthy to have it before any other competitors, among whom principally to challenge it step forth . . ."

could not abide vice by daylight, rudely clothed for to witness
outwardly their contempt of outward things, with books in
their hands against glory,[99] whereto they set their names, sophis-
tically speaking against subtlety, and angry with any man in
whom they see the foul fault of anger. These men casting lar-
gesse as they go of definitions, divisions, and distinctions,[100]
with a scornful interrogative do soberly ask whether it be possible to find any path so ready to lead a man to virtue as that
which teacheth what virtue is; and teacheth it not only by delivering forth his very being, his causes and effects, but also by
making known his enemy vice, which must be destroyed, and
his cumbersome servant passion, which must be mastered, by
showing the generalities that containeth it, and the specialities
that are derived from it; lastly, by plain setting down, how it
extendeth itself out of the limits of a man's own little world to
the government of families, and maintaining of public societies.

The historian scarcely giveth leisure to the moralist to say so
much, but that he, loaden with old mouse-eaten records, author-
izing himself (for the most part) upon other histories, whose
greatest authorities are built upon the notable foundation of
hearsay, having much ado to accord differing writers, and to
pick truth out of partiality, better acquainted with a thousand
years ago than with the present age, and yet better knowing
how this world goeth than how his own wit runneth, curious for
antiquities and inquisitive of novelties, a wonder to young folks
and a tyrant in table talk, denieth in a great chafe that any man,
for teaching of virtue and virtuous actions, is comparable to him.
I am *testis temporum, lux veritatis, vita memoriae, magistra*

[99]The moral philosophers carry books which argue against the pursuit of
personal glory. Cf. Cicero, *Tusculan Disputations*, I, xv, 34.

[100]Definitions, divisions, and distinctions are terms from medieval scholastic logic which survived in Renaissance handbooks. Definition is the most
general statement about an object, stating its genus and specific difference
(e.g., "man is a rational animal"). Division is a more specific classification
into species, parts, or adjuncts, and distinction is the separation of a substance and its accidents. See Sister Miriam Joseph, *Shakespeare's Use of the
Arts of Language* (1947), pp. 312 ff.

vitae, nuncia vetustatis.[101] The philosopher (saith he) teacheth a disputative virtue,[102] but I do an active; his virtue is excellent in the dangerless Academy of Plato,[103] but mine showeth forth her honorable face in the battles of Marathon,[104] Pharsalia,[105] Poitiers,[106] and Agincourt.[107] He teacheth virtue by certain abstract considerations, but I only bid you follow the footing of them that have gone before you. Old-aged experience goeth beyond the fine-witted philosopher, but I give the experience of many ages.[108] Lastly, if he make the song-book, I put the learner's hand to the lute; and if he be the guide, I am the light.

Then would he allege you innumerable examples, confirming story by story, how much the wisest senators and princes have been directed by the credit of history, as Brutus,[109] Alphonsus of Aragon,[110] and who not, if need be? At length the long line of their disputation maketh a point in this, that the one giveth the precept, and the other the example.

[101]"The witness of time, the light of truth, the life of memory, the directress of life, the herald of antiquity." This allusion to Cicero's *De Oratore*, II, ix, 36 would have been familiar to many of Sidney's readers. The Latin quotation is from Ponsonby. Olney's text reads (incorrectly): *"lux vitae, temporum magistra, vita memoriae, nuncia vetustatis, &c."* Norwich is almost identical to Olney.

[102]Philosophers debate over the definitions of virtues and vices, but care little for their practical application.

[103]This was Plato's school in Athens, founded about 385 B.C.

[104]The Greeks gained their first victory over the Persians at Marathon in 490 B.C.

[105]Julius Caesar defeated Pompey at Pharsalia in 48 B.C. This battle is the subject of a poem by Lucan (see n. 79, above).

[106]The English defeated the French at Poitiers in 1356.

[107]Agincourt, where Henry V defeated the French in 1415, is commemorated in Drayton's *Ballad of Agincourt*.

[108]Elyot uses this argument in *The Governor*, pp. 280 ff.

[109]Brutus (85–42 B.C.) conspired to overthrow, and finally murdered, Julius Caesar. In his *Life of Brutus*, IV, Plutarch reports that Brutus was given to long hours of reading in Polybius.

[110]Alphonsus of Aragon reigned from 1416 to 1458. Sidney garnered his materials on Alphonsus from Amyot's "To the Readers" in Sir Thomas North's translation of Plutarch's *Lives* (1579). Amyot relates that Alphonsus, fallen sick, delighted to hear "the storie of Quintus Curtius, concerning the deedes of Alexander the great."

Now whom shall we find (sith the question standeth for the highest form[111] in the school of learning) to be moderator? Truly, as me seemeth, the poet; and if not a moderator, even the man that ought to carry the title from them both, and much more from all other serving sciences. Therefore compare we the poet with the historian and with the moral philosopher, and if he go beyond them both, no other human skill can match him. For as for the divine, with all reverence it is ever to be excepted, not only for having his scope as far beyond any of these as eternity exceedeth a moment, but even for passing each of these in themselves.[112] And for the lawyer, though *jus* be the daughter of justice, and justice the chief of virtues,[113] yet because he seeketh to make men good rather *formidine poenae* than *virtutis amore*,[114] or to say righter, doth not endeavor to make men good, but that their evil hurt not others; having no care so he be a good citizen, how bad a man he be; therefore as our wickedness maketh him necessary, and necessity maketh him honorable, so is he not in the deepest truth to stand in rank with these who all endeavor to take naughtiness away, and plant goodness even in the secretest cabinet of our souls. And these four are all that any way deal in that consideration of men's manners, which being the supreme knowledge, they that best breed it deserve the best commendation.

The philosopher therefore and the historian are they which would win the goal, the one by precept, the other by example.[115]

111A form is a class in school.
112Poetry, like the rest of the arts and sciences, teaches through an appeal to human reason. Matters of divinity, however, are "to be excepted" because they fall beyond the reach of the rational faculties.
113Elyot takes this position in *The Governor*, p. 195: "And as Aristotell sayeth, justice is nat onely a portion or spice of vertue, but it is intierly the same vertue. And therof onely (sayeth Tulli) men be called good men, as who saieth that without justice all other qualities and vertues can nat make a man good." See *Nicomachean Ethics*, V, 1; and *De Officiis*, III, vi, 28.
114"Fear of punishment" and "love of virtue" (Horace, *Epistles*, I, xvi, 52–53).
115As Shepherd points out (p. 171), Sidney is here following Amyot's lead as it appears in North's Plutarch.

But both, not having both, do both halt. For the philosopher, setting down with thorny argument the bare rule, is so hard of utterance and so misty to be conceived, that one that hath no other guide but him shall wade in him till he be old before he shall find sufficient cause to be honest. For his knowledge standeth so upon the abstract and general that happy is that man who may understand him, and more happy that can apply what he doth understand.[116]

On the other side, the historian, wanting the precept, is so tied, not to what should be but to what is, to the particular truth of things and not to the general reason of things, that his example draweth no necessary consequence, and therefore a less fruitful doctrine.[117]

Now doth the peerless poet perform both: for whatsoever the philosopher saith should be done, he giveth a perfect picture of it in someone by whom he presupposeth it was done, so as he coupleth the general notion with the particular example. A perfect picture[118] I say, for he yieldeth to the powers of the mind an image of that whereof the philosopher bestoweth but a wordish description, which doth neither strike, pierce, nor possess the sight of the soul so much as that other doth. For as in outward things, to a man that had never seen an elephant or a rhinoceros, who should tell him most exquisitely all their shapes,

[116]Sidney's dispraise of scholastic subtleties is in a tradition common to Renaissance humanists. Roger Ascham, for example (Smith, I, 6), found philosophers and theologians "rude in uttering their mynde." The counter argument, that poetry succeeds where philosophy fails, is perhaps best stated in *Areopagitica*, where Milton pays tribute to "our sage and serious poet Spenser (whom I dare be known to think a better teacher than Scotus or Aquinas)."

[117]See n. 62, above. Sidney here reiterates that the universal ("the general reason of things") excels the particular for purposes of teaching. Olney reads "fruitless doctrine," but substitutes "fruitful" in his *errata*. The variant "fruitful," which appears in both Ponsonby and Norwich, is clearly correct.

[118]On the *ut pictura poesis* tradition see n. 65, above. It is noteworthy that Sidney continues to stress the visual rather than the auditory qualities of poetry. The poet transmits ideas seen in the mind through the medium of words. The reader's "inward conceits" are the final resting place of "true lively knowledge."

color, bigness, and particular marks; or of a gorgeous palace, the
architecture, with declaring the full beauties, might well make
the hearer able to repeat, as it were by rote, all he had heard, yet
should never satisfy his inward conceits with being witness to
itself of a true lively knowledge. But the same man, as soon as
he might see those beasts well painted, or the house well in
model, should straightways grow without need of any description, to a judicial comprehending of them. So no doubt the
philosopher, with his learned definition,[119] be it of virtue, vices,
matters of public policy or private government, replenisheth the
memory with many infallible grounds of wisdom, which, notwithstanding, lie dark before the imaginative and judging power
if they be not illuminated or figured forth by the speaking picture of poesy.

Tully taketh much pains and many times not without poetical
helps to make us know the force love of our country hath in
us.[120] Let us but hear old Anchises speaking in the midst of
Troy's flames,[121] or see Ulysses in the fulness of all Calypso's
delights bewail his absence from barren and beggarly Ithaca.[122]
Anger, the Stoics say, was a short madness:[123] let but Sophocles[124] bring you Ajax on a stage, killing and whipping sheep and
oxen, thinking them the army of Greeks with their chieftains
Agamemnon and Menelaus, and tell me if you have not a more
familiar insight into anger than finding in the schoolmen his
genus and difference.[125] See whether wisdom and temperance

---

[119]The "wordish description."

[120]Cicero (Tully) put great stock in the examples of Greek and Roman
history as an incitement to patriotism. Sidney may be referring here to *De
Officiis*, I, xxiv, 84, where Cicero praises self-sacrifice for one's country, and
quotes Ennius as a "poetical" help.

[121]Anchises, Aeneas' father, refuses to leave Troy. See *Aeneid*, II, 634 ff.

[122]*Odyssey*, V, 149 ff.

[123]Seneca says as much, though in greater detail, in *De Ira*, I, 1, 2 ff.

[124]Sophocles (ca. 496–406 B.C.) was a Greek playwright. As Shepherd
notes (p. 173), it is unlikely that Sidney knew his play *Ajax*, for the killing
and whipping are there reported rather than acted out on stage.

[125]See n. 100, above.

in Ulysses and Diomedes, valor in Achilles, friendship in Nisus and Euryalus,[126] even to an ignorant man, carry not an apparent shining; and contrarily, the remorse of conscience in Oedipus, the soon repenting pride in Agamemnon, the self-devouring cruelty in his father Atreus,[127] the violence of ambition in the two Theban brothers,[128] the sour-sweetness of revenge in Medea;[129] and to fall lower, the Terentian Gnatho[130] and our Chaucer's Pandar,[131] so expressed that we now use their names to signify their trades; and finally, all virtues, vices, and passions so in their own natural seats laid to the view that we seem not to hear of them, but clearly to see through them.

But even in the most excellent determination of goodness, what philosopher's counsel can so readily direct a prince as the feigned Cyrus in Xenophon,[132] or a virtuous man in all fortunes, as Aeneas in Virgil, or a whole commonwealth, as the way of Sir Thomas More's *Utopia*?[133] I say the way, because where Sir Thomas More erred, it was the fault of the man and not of the poet, for that way of patterning a commonwealth was most absolute, though he perchance hath not so absolutely performed it.[134] For the question is, whether the feigned image of poesy or the regular instruction of philosophy hath the more

[126]Nisus and Euryalus were devoted friends and followers of Aeneas who died together in an attack on the Rutulian camp (*Aeneid*, IX, 433 ff.).

[127]Atreus served up to his brother, Thyestes, the flesh of the latter's children. The story appears in Aeschylus' *Agamemnon*, named after the son of Atreus.

[128]The Theban brothers were Polynices and Eteocles, who died in the battle that resulted from their quarrel over Thebes.

[129]When Jason deserts her, Medea revenges herself by murdering the children she bore him.

[130]Gnatho, the type of the parasite, appears in Terence's *Eunuch*.

[131]Pandar, the type of the pander, is from Chaucer's *Troilus and Criseyde*.

[132]See n. 59, above.

[133]First printed in Latin, the *Utopia* was translated by Ralph Robinson in 1551.

[134]Sidney's portrait of "the whole Arte of governement" in Evarchus (see n. 62, above) is evidence that he would not have agreed with the communistic political ideal presented in *Utopia*.

force in teaching: wherein if the philosophers have more rightly showed themselves philosophers than the poets have obtained to the high top of their profession, as in truth,

> *Mediocribus esse poetis,*
> *Non dii, non homines, non concessere columnae;*[135]

it is, I say again, not the fault of the art, but that by few men that art can be accomplished.

Certainly, even our Saviour Christ could as well have given the moral commonplaces of uncharitableness and humbleness as the divine narration of Dives and Lazarus;[136] or of disobedience and mercy, as that heavenly discourse of the lost child and the gracious father;[137] but that His through-searching wisdom knew the estate of Dives burning in hell, and of Lazarus being in Abraham's bosom, would more constantly (as it were) inhabit both the memory and judgment. Truly, for myself, me seems I see before my eyes the lost child's disdainful prodigality, turned to envy a swine's dinner: which by the learned divines are thought not historical acts, but instructing parables.[138] For conclusion, I say the philosopher teacheth, but he teacheth obscurely, so as the learned only can understand him; that is to say, he teacheth them that are already taught. But the poet is the food for the tenderest stomachs, the poet is indeed the right popular philosopher, whereof Aesop's tales give good proof; whose pretty allegories, stealing under the formal tales of beasts, make many more beastly than beasts begin to hear the sound of virtue from these dumb speakers.[139]

135"Neither gods, nor men, nor booksellers, tolerate mediocrity in poets" (Horace, *Ars Poetica*, 372–73).

136Luke 16:20–31.

137Sidney is referring to the parable of the prodigal son, in Luke 15:11–32.

138The notion that the methods of the Bible and of poetry were similar was not uncommon among writers before and during the Renaissance. For example, cf. Boccaccio's *Life of Dante* (Gilbert, pp. 208 ff.).

139Like parables from the Bible, allegorical tales teach by vivid exemplification rather than bald definition. Aesop's *Fables* were very popular during the Renaissance, both for their "delightful teaching" and as an introduction to Greek. Elyot (*The Governor*, pp. 35–36), for example, recommends that

But now may it be alleged that if this imagining of matters be so fit for the imagination, then must the historian needs surpass, who bringeth you images of true matters, such as indeed were done, and not such as fantastically or falsely may be suggested to have been done.[140] Truly, Aristotle himself, in his discourse of poesy, plainly determineth this question, saying that poetry is *philosophoteron* and *spoudaioteron*, that is to say, it is more philosophical and more studiously serious than history. His reason is, because poesy dealeth with *katholou*, that is to say, with the universal consideration, and the history with *kathekaston*, the particular: now, saith he, the universal weighs what is fit to be said or done, either in likelihood or necessity (which the poesy considereth in his imposed names), and the particular only marks whether Alcibiades did or suffered this or that.[141] Thus far Aristotle, which reason of his (as all his) is most full of reason.

For indeed, if the question were whether it were better to have a particular act truly or falsely set down, there is no doubt which is to be chosen, no more than whether you had rather have Vespasian's[142] picture right as he was, or at the painter's pleasure, nothing resembling. But if the question be for your own use and

---

children should hear "Esopes fables in greke: in whiche argument children moche do delite. And surely it is a moche pleasant lesson and also profitable, as well for that it is elegant and brefe, (and nat withstanding it hath moche varietie in wordes, and therwith moche helpeth to the understandinge of greke) as also in those fables is included moche morall and politike wisedome." For the same argument in Italian poetics, see Weinberg, I, 202.

[140]See n. 298, below.

[141]*Poetics*, IX. Sidney's remarks here are completely consistent with what he has laid down in previous passages. See n. 55 and n. 62, above. By "imposed names" Sidney means (with Aristotle) names that will indicate the universality of the poetic personages. The *Arcadia* is populated with a variety of such types: Basilius ("ruler"), Pamela ("all sweetness"), Philoclea ("lover of glory") are examples, and *Astrophil and Stella* ("Star-lover and Star") follows the same rule. For a list of the Arcadian names, see *Poems*, p. 382.

Olney reads, "and the particular, only mark, whether Alcibiades did, or suffered, this or that." But he substitutes "marks" for "mark" in his *errata*. Both Ponsonby and Norwich read "marketh."

[142]Vespasian, an emperor of Rome, was born A.D. 9 and ruled A.D. 69–79.

idealized art

learning, whether it be better to have it set down as it should be
or as it was, then certainly is more doctrinable the feigned Cyrus
in Xenophon[143] than the true Cyrus in Justin,[144] and the feigned
Aeneas in Virgil than the right Aeneas in Dares Phrygius.[145] As
to a lady that desired to fashion her countenance to the best
grace, a painter should more benefit her to portrait a most sweet
face, writing Canidia[146] upon it, than to paint Canidia as she
was, who Horace sweareth was foul and ill favored.[147]

If the poet do his part aright, he will show you in Tantalus,[148]
Atreus,[149] and such like, nothing that is not to be shunned; in
Cyrus,[150] Aeneas, Ulysses, each thing to be followed; where the
historian, bound to tell things as things were, cannot be liberal
(without he will be poetical) of a perfect pattern,[151] but as in
Alexander[152] or Scipio[153] himself, show doings, some to be

[143]See n. 59, above.

[144]Justin (third century A.D.) produced an epitome of Pompeius Trogus'
Historiae Philippicae, which was translated into English by Arthur Golding
in 1564. Justin's portrait of Cyrus is short, in some respects critical, and
much less imposing than Xenophon's.

[145]Dares Phrygius, mentioned in *Iliad*, V, 9, was the author of a work
known as *De Exicidio Trojae*, which purported to be a Latin translation of
a lost account of the Trojan War. The work was very popular during the
Middle Ages (cf. Chaucer, *Troilus and Criseyde*, I, 146).

[146]Olney reads "Candida," but corrects the error in his *errata*. "Canidia"
appears in both Ponsonby and Norwich.

[147]Canidia, a courtesan, ignored Horace's affections, and thereby earned
the ghastly portrait he draws in *Epodes*, V. Cf. also *Epodes*, XVII; and
Satires, I, viii, 23 ff.

[148]Tantalus was a legendary king of great wealth. He divulged the secrets
entrusted to him by the gods and was punished with a terrible hunger and
thirst, both of which remained forever unsatisfied.

[149]See n. 127, above.

[150]See n. 59, above.

[151]Limited to relating things as they actually happened, the historian
cannot ennoble his materials ("cannot be liberal") through the use of the
universal ("a perfect pattern") without becoming "poetical."

[152]A pupil of Aristotle and admirer of Homer, Alexander "the Great" of
Macedonia (356–323 B.C.) succeeded to the throne of his own country at the
age of twenty, and in the thirteen years before his death distinguished himself as the greatest general of antiquity. Ancient historians were divided in
their views of Alexander. Some praised him as a hero, and others, such as
Quintus Curtius, were less favorable.

[153]See n. 328, below.

liked, some to be misliked. And then how will you discern what to follow but by your own discretion, which you had without reading Quintus Curtius? And whereas a man may say, though in universal consideration of doctrine the poet prevaileth, yet that the history, in his saying such a thing was done, doth warrant a man more in that he shall follow. The answer is manifest, that if he stand upon that was, as if he should argue, because it rained yesterday, therefore it should rain today, then indeed it hath some advantage to a gross conceit.[154] But if he know an example only informs[155] a conjectured likelihood, and so go by reason, the poet doth so far exceed him, as he is to frame his example to that which is most reasonable, be it in warlike, politic, or private matters; where the historian in his bare was hath many times that which we call fortune to overrule the best wisdom. Many times he[156] must tell events whereof he can yield no cause; or if he do, it must be poetical.

For that a feigned example hath as much force to teach as a true example (for as for to move, it is clear, sith the feigned may be tuned to the highest key of passion), let us take one example wherein a poet and a historian do concur. Herodotus and Justin do both testify that Zopyrus,[157] King Darius' faithful servant, seeing his master long resisted by the rebellious Babylonians, feigned himself in extreme disgrace of his king, for verifying of which he caused his own nose and ears to be cut off: and so flying to the Babylonians, was received, and for his known valor so far credited that he did find means to deliver them over to Darius. Much like matter doth Livy record of Tarquinius and his son.[158] Xenophon excellently feigneth such another stratagem performed by Abradatas in Cyrus' behalf.[159]

[154]Someone easily convinced.

[155]Norwich: "confirms."

[156]The historian.

[157]The exploits of Zopyrus are related by Justin (*Histories*, I, x) and by Herodotus (*History*, III, 153–60).

[158]Livy (*Histories*, I, liii–liv) records that Sextus, the son of Tarquin the Proud, deserted to the enemy, and then, having succeeded in his deception, used his position to his father's advantage.

[159]In Xenophon's *Cyropaedia*, VI, i, 45–48, Abradatas transfers his allegiance from the Assyrian king to Cyrus, the leader of the Persians. But, as

Now would I fain know, if occasion be presented unto you to serve your prince by such an honest dissimulation, why you do not as well learn it of Xenophon's fiction as of the other's verity? And truly so much the better, as you shall save your nose by the bargain, for Abradatas did not counterfeit so far. So then the best of the historian is subject to the poet; for whatsoever action or faction, whatsoever counsel, policy, or war stratagem the historian is bound to recite, that may the poet (if he list) with his imitation make his own, beautifying it both for further teaching and more delighting, as it pleaseth him: having all, from Dante his heaven to his hell,[160] under the authority of his pen. Which if I be asked what poets have done so, as I might well name some, yet say I, and say again, I speak of the art and not of the artificer.[161]

Now, to that which commonly is attributed to the praise of histories, in respect of the notable learning is gotten by marking the success, as though therein a man should see virtue exalted and vice punished;[162] truly that commendation is peculiar to poetry, and far off from history. For indeed poetry ever setteth virtue so out in her best colors, making fortune her well-waiting handmaid, that one must needs be enamored of her. Well may you see Ulysses in a storm[163] and in other hard plights, but they are but exercises of patience and magnanimity, to make them shine the more in the near-following prosperity. And of the contrary part, if evil men come to the stage, they ever go out (as the tragedy writer[164] answered to one that misliked the show of

---

Sidney says, Abradatas "did not counterfeit so far" as Zopyrus or Sextus. For another interpretation, see Shepherd, p. 178.

[160]*The Divine Comedy*, with its tripartite division between *Inferno*, *Purgatorio*, and *Paradiso*, quite literally fulfills Sidney's description.

[161]See p. 23, above.

[162]Sir Thomas Elyot, for example, states (*The Governor*, pp. 280–81) "that there is no doctrine, be it eyther divine or humaine, that is nat eyther all expressed in historie or at the leste mixte with historie."

[163]*Odyssey*, V, 291 ff.

[164]According to Plutarch (*Moralia, How to Study Poetry*, 4), Euripides (fifth century B.C.) used such an argument.

such persons) so manacled as they little animate folks to follow them. But the historian, being captived to the truth of a foolish world, is many times a terror from well doing, and an encouragement to unbridled wickedness. For see we not valiant Miltiades[165] rot in his fetters; the just Phocion[166] and the accomplished Socrates put to death like traitors; the cruel Severus[167] live prosperously; the excellent Severus[168] miserably murdered; Sylla and Marius[169] dying in their beds; Pompey[170] and Cicero[171] slain then, when they would have thought exile a happiness? See we not virtuous Cato[172] driven to kill himself, and rebel Caesar so advanced that his name yet after 1600 years lasteth in the highest honor? And mark but even Caesar's own words of the fore-named Sylla[173] (who in that only did honestly, to put down his dishonest tyranny), *literas nescivit,*[174] as if want of learning caused him to do well. He meant it not by poetry, which not

[165]Miltiades (ca. 550–489 B.C.) was an Athenian leader who won a decisive victory on the fields of Marathon. In spite of his victory, however, Miltiades ended his life in an Athenian prison.

[166]Phocion, an Athenian general and statesman, was condemned to death for his political views in 318 B.C. Plutarch's *Life of Phocion* is the portrayal of an upright and patriotic leader.

[167]Lucius Septimus Severus, Roman Emperor A.D. 193–211, was a calculating soldier and politician who died while leading an invasion of Britain.

[168]Alexander Severus, Roman Emperor A.D. 222–35, was a gentle though ineffectual leader who was murdered by his rebellious troops.

[169]Caius Marius and Lucius Sylla were rival generals and politicians in Rome during the late second and early first centuries B.C. Marius was a leader in the popular party, and his jealousy of Sylla, later a ruthless dictator, precipitated a long and bloody conflict.

[170]Pompey (106–48 B.C.) was mastered by Caesar in the battle at Pharsalia; he fled to Egypt, where he was stabbed to death.

[171]Cicero (106–43 B.C.), who was precariously involved in Roman politics during most of his adult life, took the side of the Republicans after the murder of Caesar in 44 B.C. But with the formation of a new triumvirate in 43 B.C., Cicero's life was in mortal jeopardy. He attempted to escape, but was overtaken and executed.

[172]Cato (95–46 B.C.) was a Roman aristocrat and Stoic who took his own life when opposition to Julius Caesar proved futile; he was called "Uticensis" after Utica, the place of his death.

[173]See n. 169, above.

[174]"He was ignorant of letters." Cook points out (p. 89) that Caesar's remarks are recorded in Suetonius' *Julius Caesar.*

content with earthly plagues, deviseth new punishments in hell
for tyrants, nor yet by philosophy, which teacheth *occidendos
esse*;[175] but no doubt by skill in history, for that indeed can
afford you Cypselus,[176] Periander,[177] Phalaris,[178] Dionysius,[179]
and I know not how many more of the same kennel, that speed
well enough in their abominable unjustice or usurpation. I con-
clude therefore, that he excelleth history, not only in furnishing
the mind with knowledge, but in setting it forward to that which
deserveth to be called and accounted good: which setting forward and moving to well doing indeed setteth the laurel crown
upon the poet as victorious, not only of the historian, but over
the philosopher, howsoever in teaching it may be question-
able.[180]

For suppose it be granted (that which I suppose with great

[175]"They are to be killed." Plato's intense hatred of despotism is well
illustrated in *The Republic*, VIII–IX. Cicero (*De Officiis*, III, vi, 32 and
III, xxi, 83) contends that tyrannicide is justified because the tyrant de-
stroys the natural bond between men in society. An even more extreme
view is taken by More's Utopians. See Robert P. Adams, *The Better Part
of Valor* (1962), pp. 155–57.

[176]Cypselus was a tyrant (i.e., Greek term for ruler) of Corinth who
ruled for about thirty years until 625 B.C.

[177]Periander was the son of Cypselus and, like his father, the tyrant of
Corinth. He ruled from about 625 to 585 B.C.

[178]Phalaris was a notoriously cruel tyrant (ca. 570–544 B.C.) of Acragas
(in Sicily).

[179]Dionysius the Elder (ca. 430–367 B.C.) was a tyrant of Syracuse.

[180]In allowing the philosopher possible superiority in teaching, Sidney
is making only a temporary concession. As he proceeds in his argument it
will become clear that the poet's teaching has a practical result in the positive moral disposition of the reader, and that such a result can occur only
when teaching is augmented by moving and delight. In general delight is
the power of capturing and sustaining the interest of an audience, while
moving has persuasion to a life of active virtue as its effect. The distinction
between teaching and moving and delighting was familiar during the Renaissance, and represents an elaboration of Horace's famous division of the
ends of poetry into the profitable and the pleasurable (*Ars Poetica*, 333 ff.).
Characteristically, Sidney's discussion implies a separation between the
powers and functions of the intellect and will. Left to itself, the intellect
is merely an inert receptacle for knowledge, and requires the energy and
direction of the will in order to make it morally functional. It is the capacity
to activate and direct his reader's will through teaching and delight that
constitutes the poet's superiority over the philosopher. See n. 83, above.

reason may be denied) that the philosopher, in respect of his
methodical proceeding, doth teach more perfectly than the poet:
yet do I think that no man is so much *philophilosophos*[181] as to
compare the philosopher in moving with the poet. And that
moving is of a higher degree than teaching, it may by this appear: that it is well nigh the cause and the effect of teaching.
For who will be taught if he be not moved with desire to be
taught; and what so much good doth that teaching bring forth
(I speak still of moral doctrine) as that it moveth one to do
that which it doth teach? For as Aristotle saith, it is not *gnosis*
but *praxis* must be the fruit.[182] And how *praxis* can be,[183] without being moved to practice, is no hard matter to consider.

The philosopher showeth you the way, he informeth you of
the particularities, as well of the tediousness of the way, as of
the pleasant lodging you shall have when your journey is ended,
as of the many by-turnings that may divert you from your way.
But this is to no man but to him that will read him, and read
him with attentive studious painfulness; which constant desire,
whosoever hath in him, hath already passed half the hardness of
the way, and therefore is beholding to the philosopher but for
the other half. Nay truly, learned men have learnedly thought
that where once reason hath so much overmastered passion as
that the mind hath a free desire to do well, the inward light
each mind hath in itself is as good as a philosopher's book;[184]
seeing in nature we know it is well to do well, and what is well
and what is evil, although not in the words of art[185] which
philosophers bestow upon us; for out of natural conceit[186] the

[181]"Lover of philosophers."

[182]*Gnosis* is "knowledge"; *praxis* is "practice" or "action." The reference
is to Aristotle's *Nicomachean Ethics*, I, 3.

[183]Olney reads "cannot," but the variant "can," which appears in both
Ponsonby and Norwich, is obviously correct.

[184]See n. 249, below.

[185]"Words of art" refers to the elaborate technical vocabulary of the
scholastic philosophers.

[186]By "natural conceit" Sidney means concepts derived from nature as
they appear in the mind. The distinction here is between concepts in their
natural form, seen in the mind, and concepts artificially set forth in words.
See n. 65, above.

philosophers drew it. But to be moved to do that which we know, or to be moved with desire to know, *hoc opus, hic labor est*.[187]

Now therein of all sciences (I speak still of human, and according to the human conceits) is our poet the monarch. For he doth not only show the way, but giveth so sweet a prospect into the way, as will entice any man to enter into it. Nay, he doth as if your journey should lie through a fair vineyard, at the first give you a cluster of grapes, that full of that taste, you may long to pass further. He beginneth not with obscure definitions which must blur the margent with interpretations and load the memory with doubtfulness, but he cometh to you with words set in delightful proportion, either accompanied with, or prepared for, the well enchanting skill of music; and with a tale forsooth he cometh unto you, with a tale which holdeth children from play and old men from the chimney corner. And pretending no more,[188] doth intend the winning of the mind from wickedness to virtue, even as the child is often brought to take most wholesome things by hiding them in such other as have a pleasant taste: which, if one should begin to tell them the nature of aloes or rhubarb[189] they should receive, would sooner take their physic at their ears than at their mouth. So is it in men (most of which are childish in the best things till they be cradled in their graves), glad they will be to hear the tales of Hercules, Achilles, Cyrus,[190] and Aeneas; and hearing them, must needs hear the right description of wisdom, valor, and justice; which, if they had been barely, that is to say, philosophically set out, they would swear they be brought to school again.

That imitation whereof poetry is, hath the most conveniency to nature of all other, insomuch that, as Aristotle saith, those things which in themselves are horrible, as cruel battles, un-

187"This is the task, this is the labor" (*Aeneid*, VI, 129).
188Making no greater claim than to be a tale.
189Aloes and rhubarb are generic names for plants notable for their bitterness which were often used as purgatives during the period in which Sidney lived.
190See n. 59, above.

natural monsters, are made in poetical imitation delightful.[191]
Truly, I have known men that, even with reading *Amadis de
Gaule*[192] (which God knoweth wanteth much of a perfect
poesy), have found their hearts moved to the exercise of cour-
tesy, liberality, and especially courage. Who readeth Aeneas
carrying old Anchises on his back[193] that wisheth not it were his
fortune to perform so excellent an act? Whom do not the words
of Turnus move (the tale of Turnus having planted his image
in the imagination)?

> *Fugientem haec terra videbit,*
> *Usque adeone mori miserum est?*[194]

Where the philosophers, as they scorn to delight, so must they
be content little to move, saving wrangling whether virtue be
the chief or the only good, whether the contemplative or the
active life do excel:[195] which Plato and Boethius well knew,[196]
and therefore made mistress philosophy very often borrow the

---

[191]Aristotle argues (*Poetics*, IV) that all men take delight in imitation,
and defends his assertion with the observation that people generally enjoy
the accurate representation of things that would cause them displeasure if
observed in actuality. Sidney, while concerned to show that we can enjoy
in art what would repel us in fact, is not locating the source of that pleasure
in the artist's imitative proficiency. Rather, judging from his examples, he
seems to mean that poetic descriptions of horrible monsters and cruel battles are delightful because they are occasions for the illustration of virtuous
behavior. For a different reading, see Shepherd, p. 183.

[192]*Amadis de Gaule* was a late fifteenth-century Spanish redaction of a
now lost medieval romance. The story of Amadis, a flourishing chivalric
hero, was available to Sidney in a French translation of 1540.

[193]*Aeneid*, II, 705 ff.

[194]"Shall this land see Turnus in flight? Is it such a terrible thing to
die?" (*Aeneid*, XII, 645–46). Turnus, the king of the Rutulians and suitor
of Lavinia, pursues a losing war against the Trojans, and is finally overcome
by Aeneas.

[195]These are perpetual philosophical questions.

[196]As Ascham remarks in *The Schoolmaster* (Smith, I, 21), in the best
teaching the dry precepts of Aristotle should be supplemented with the
lively examples to be found in Plato. Sidney has already remarked (p. 8,
above) on Plato's use of fables. In his celebrated *Consolation of Philosophy*
(ca. 520 A.D.), a treatise written in prison before his execution, Boethius
alternates between prose and verse.

masking raiment of poesy. For even those hard-hearted evil men
who think virtue a school name,[197] and know no other good but
indulgere genio,[198] and therefore despise the austere admoni-
tions of the philosopher, and feel not the inward reason they
stand upon, yet will be content to be delighted, which is all the
good fellow poet seemeth to promise, and so steal to see the
form of goodness (which seen they cannot but love) ere themselves be aware, as if they took a medicine of cherries.

Infinite proofs of the strange effects of this poetical invention
might be alleged; only two shall serve, which are so often remembered as I think all men know them. The one of Menenius
Agrippa,[199] who, when the whole people of Rome had reso-
lutely divided themselves from the Senate, with apparent show
of utter ruin, though he were (for that time) an excellent orator, came not among them upon trust of figurative speeches or
cunning insinuations, and much less with far fet maxims of
philosophy, which (especially if they were Platonic) they must
have learned geometry before they could well have conceived;[200]
but forsooth he behaves himself like a homely[201] and familiar
poet. He telleth them a tale, that there was a time when all the
parts of the body made a mutinous conspiracy against the belly,
which they thought devoured the fruits of each other's labor:
they concluded they would let so unprofitable a spender starve.
In the end, to be short (for the tale is notorious, and as notorious that it was a tale), with punishing the belly they plagued

197It was a commonplace among the humanists that the Schoolmen (the
medieval Scholastic philosophers) spent too much time quibbling over
nominal distinctions, and too little encouraging practical virtue. For a more
elaborate example of his penchant for *praxis*, see Sidney's letter to his
brother Robert (*Works*, III, 130–33).

198"Indulge your desires" (Persius, *Satires*, V, 151).

199The story has been well known since antiquity, though it is perhaps
most familiar to modern readers in Shakespeare's *Coriolanus*. For a full
background, see the New Variorum ed. of *Coriolanus*, ed. H. H. Furness,
Jr. (1928), pp. 39–41.

200Plato's preoccupation with numbers, particularly in *The Republic* and
Timaeus, gave credence to the notion, commonly held in the Renaissance,
that the Academy was closed to all but those who understood geometry.

201"Homely" here means "natural."

themselves. This applied by him wrought such effect in the people, as I never read that ever[202] words brought forth but then so sudden and so good an alteration; for upon reasonable conditions a perfect reconcilement ensued.[203] The other is of Nathan the prophet,[204] who when the holy David had so far forsaken God as to confirm adultery with murder, when he was to do the tenderest office of a friend, in laying his own shame before his eyes, sent by God to call again so chosen a servant, how doth he it but by telling of a man whose beloved lamb was ungratefully taken from his bosom?—the application most divinely true, but the discourse itself feigned; which made David (I speak of the second and instrumental cause[205]), as in a glass, to see his own filthiness, as that heavenly psalm of mercy[206] well testifieth.

By these therefore examples and reasons I think it may be manifest that the poet, with that same hand of delight, doth draw the mind more effectually than any other art doth. And so a conclusion not unfitly ensueth, that as virtue is the most excellent resting place for all worldly learning to make his end of, so poetry, being the most familiar to teach it, and most princely to move towards it, in the most excellent work is the most excellent workman.

But I am content not only to decipher him by his works (although works in commendation or dispraise must ever hold an high authority), but more narrowly will examine his parts, so that (as in a man), though all together may carry a presence full of majesty and beauty, perchance in some one defectious piece we may find a blemish. Now in his parts, kinds, or species (as you list to term them), it is to be noted that some poesies have

[202]Both Ponsonby and Norwich read "only."

[203]Evarchus compares the state to a body, and with equal success, in *Arcadia* (*Works*, I, 187).

[204]Nathan's parable, which forces David to recognize his own sins against the Lord, and which results in the death of one of David's children, appears in II Samuel 12.

[205]The second cause is the parable itself, while the first cause of David's repentance is the will of God.

[206]Psalm 51, in which David prays for the remission of his sins.

coupled together two or three kinds, as tragical and comical, whereupon is risen the tragi-comical.[207] Some, in the like manner, have mingled prose and verse, as Sannazzaro[208] and Boethius.[209] Some have mingled matters heroical and pastoral.[210] But that cometh all to one in this question, for if severed they be good, the conjunction cannot be hurtful. Therefore, perchance forgetting some, and leaving some as needless to be remembered, it shall not be amiss in a word to cite the special kinds, to see what faults may be found in the right use of them.

Is it then the pastoral poem which is misliked (for perchance where the hedge is lowest they will soonest leap over)?[211] Is the poor pipe disdained which sometime out of Meliboeus'[212] mouth can show the misery of people under hard lords or ravening soldiers? And again, by Tityrus,[212] what blessedness is derived to them that lie lowest from the goodness of them that sit highest? sometimes, under the pretty tales of wolves and sheep,[213]

[207]On tragi-comedy, see n. 411, below.

[208]Jacopo Sannazzaro (1458–1530) of Naples, whose *Arcadia* was published at the beginning of the sixteenth century, initiated the subsequent rage for pastoral romances with interspersed verse eclogues. Sannazzaro provided Sidney with a standard for his evaluation of English pastoral poetry (see pp. 62–63, below), and was also a model for Sidney's *Arcadia*. For Sannazzaro's influence on Sidney, see David Kalstone, *Sidney's Poetry* (1965), chs. 1 and 3. The question of whether prose could be included in the same category with poetry was a burning one for Renaissance theorists, particularly in Italy. See Baxter Hathaway, *The Age of Criticism* (1962), ch. 6.

[209]See n. 196, above.

[210]Again Sannazzaro's *Arcadia* fits the description, as does Sidney's *Arcadia*.

[211]Like most Renaissance poets, Sidney thinks of the pastoral as the humblest of the poetic genres, designed for low subjects and to be executed in an equally low style. The pastoral tradition takes its roots in the *Idylls* of the Greek poet Theocritus, though for Sidney's generation the example of Virgil's *Eclogues* bore greater weight. Partly in response to continental influences, English poets often converted the pastoral into a forum for social and religious commentary. Cf., for example, Spenser's *Shepherd's Calendar* and Milton's *Lycidas*.

[212]Meliboeus appears in Virgil, *Eclogues*, I, where he complains of his enforced flight from his homeland, while Tityrus, Virgil himself, expands reverently upon the virtues of Rome.

[213]Cf. Spenser, *Shepherd's Calendar*, September Eclogue.

can include the whole considerations of wrong doing and patience; sometimes show that contention for trifles can get but
a trifling victory; where perchance a man may see that even
Alexander and Darius,[214] when they strave who should be cock
of this world's dunghill, the benefit they got was that the after-
livers may say,

> Haec memini et victum frustra contendere Thirsin:
> Ex illo Corydon, Corydon est tempore nobis.[215]

Or is it the lamenting elegiac?[216] which in a kind heart would
move rather pity than blame, who bewails with the great philosopher Heraclitus[217] the weakness of mankind and the wretch-
edness of the world; who surely is to be praised, either for
compassionate accompanying just causes of lamentation, or for
rightly painting out how weak be the passions of woefulness. Is
it the bitter but wholesome iambic?[218] which rubs the galled
mind in making shame the trumpet of villainy with bold and
open crying out against naughtiness. Or the satiric? who

> Omne vafer vitium, ridenti tangit amico;[219]

who sportingly never leaveth until he make a man laugh at folly,
and at length ashamed to laugh at himself, which he cannot
avoid, without avoiding the folly; who, while

[214]Alexander (for details see n. 152, above) defeated Darius (ca. 380–
330 B.C.), the cowardly king of Persia, on two occasions before the latter
was finally murdered by his own soldiers.
[215]"These things I remember, that the conquered Thyrsis contended in
vain. Henceforth Corydon, Corydon is ours" (Virgil, Eclogues, VII, 69–70).
[216]Although the Latin elegy was defined by its special meter, elegiac
poets very often wrote on amorous themes (as in Ovid's Amores). In English poetry the metrical distinction was lost, the association with love was
partially retained (as in Donne's Elegies), though the limits of the genre
were expanded to include any serious poem on love or death.
[217]Heraclitus (fl. 500 B.C.) of Ephesus, famous for his conviction that
all things are in a state of constant flux, condemned the human condition
(as Puttenham observes, Arte, p. 112) "with teares."
[218]Aristotle (Poetics, IV) associates verse in iambic meters with lower
types of poetry, particularly with satire and invective. By "wholesome" Sidney means "usefully corrective."

Circum praecordia ludit,[219]

giveth us to feel how many head-aches a passionate life bringeth
us to; how, when all is done,

Est Ulubris, animus si nos non deficit aequus.[220]

No, perchance it is the comic, whom naughty play-makers and
stage-keepers have justly made odious.[221] To the argument of
abuse I will answer after.[222] Only thus much now is to be said,
that the comedy is an imitation of the common errors of our
life, which he representeth in the most ridiculous and scornful
sort that may be, so as it is impossible that any beholder can be
content to be such a one.

Now, as in geometry the oblique must be known as well as
the right, and in arithmetic the odd as well as the even, so in
the actions of our life who seeth not the filthiness of evil wanteth
a great foil to perceive the beauty of virtue.[223] This doth the

---

[219]This quotation is adapted from Persius' description (*Satires*, I, 116–17)
of Horace's satirical method: Horace, "the rascal, probes his friend's every
fault while making him laugh; once inside he toys with his most secret
feelings."

[220]"With a firm and even mind one can achieve happiness even in an
out-of-the-way town like Ulubrae" (rendered freely) (Horace, *Epistles*, I,
xi, 30).

[221]Since antiquity, comedy had been placed on one of the lower levels
of the literary hierarchy. Aristotle, for example, regarded it as a development out of satire (*Poetics*, IV), while Boccaccio, following Horace, distinguished comedy from tragedy by its humble style (Gilbert, p. 204). Sidney, however, was one among many who assaulted the public theatres of
the times. While the Puritan attack, led by men like Stephen Gosson (see
Introduction), was a sweeping and uncritical denunciation, Sidney was
aware of abuses but nevertheless hopeful that they could be reformed. For
more detail and a reply to Gosson, see Smith, I, xiv–xvii, xxx, 61–86.

[222]See pp. 58 ff., below.

[223]The notion that comedy teaches virtue by exposing the deformities of
vice was not unprecedented. Cf., for example, Trissino (Gilbert, p. 224);
Scaliger, *Poetices*, III, 97; and Elyot, *The Governor*, p. 58: "First, comedies,
whiche they suppose to be a doctrinall of rybaudrie, they be undoubtedly
a picture or as it were a mirrour of man's life, wherin ivell is nat taught
but discovered; to the intent that men beholdynge the promptnes of youth
unto vice, and snares of harlotts and baudes laide for yonge myndes, the
disceipte of servantes, the chaunces of fortune contrary to mennes expec-
tation, they beinge therof warned may prepare them selfe to resist or pre-
vente occasion."

comedy handle so in our private and domestical matters, as with hearing it we get as it were an experience what is to be looked for of a niggardly Demea, of a crafty Davus, of a flattering Gnatho, of a vainglorious Thraso;[224] and not only to know what effects are to be expected, but to know who be such by the signifying badge[225] given them by the comedian. And little reason hath any man to say that men learn evil by seeing it so set out, sith, as I said before, there is no man living but, by the force truth hath in nature, no sooner seeth these men play their parts, but wisheth them *in pistrinum*;[226] although perchance the sack of his own faults lie so behind his back that he seeth not himself dance the same measure; whereto yet nothing can more open his eyes than to find his own actions contemptibly set forth. So that the right use of comedy will (I think) by nobody be blamed, and much less of the high and excellent tragedy, that openeth the greatest wounds and showeth forth the ulcers that are covered with tissue; that maketh kings fear to be tyrants, and tyrants manifest their tyrannical humors; that with stirring the affects[227] of admiration and commiseration teacheth the uncertainty of this world, and upon how weak foundations gilden roofs are builded;[228] that maketh us know,

[224]Demea, Davus, Gnatho, and Thraso are low "type" characters in the comedies of Terence.

[225]A character's "signifying badge" was his name (see n. 141, above), dress, manner, and other characteristics. In naming and describing the low characters in *Arcadia*, Sidney emulated the dramatists. Our initial impressions of Dametas and his family, for example, create very definite expectations: "This loutish clowne [Dametas] is such, that you never saw so ill favourd a visar; his behaviour such, that he is beyond the degree of ridiculous; and for his apparrel, even as I would wish him: *Miso* his wife, so handsome a beldame, that onely her face and her splayfoote have made her accused for a witch. . . . Betweene these two personages . . . is issued forth mistresse *Mopsa*, a fitte woman to participate of both their perfections" (*Works*, I, 21). Furthermore, there was a strong rhetorical tradition which aligned specific gestures and manners of speech with equally specific character types. Cf. Abraham Fraunce, *The Arcadian Rhetorike*, ed. Ethel Seaton (1950), pp. 196 ff.; and Shepherd, pp. 188–89.

[226]"In the mill," where recalcitrant slaves were punished with hard labor.

[227]Passions or affections.

[228]Sidney's conception of tragedy represents a confluence of various influences and traditions. That tragedy is "high and excellent" is an idea

> *Qui sceptra saevus duro imperio regit,*
> *Timet timentes, metus in auctorem redit.*[229]

But how much it can move, Plutarch yieldeth a notable testimony of the abominable tyrant Alexander Phaeraeus,[230] from whose eyes a tragedy well made and represented drew abundance of tears; who without all pity had murdered infinite numbers, and some of his own blood, so as he that was not ashamed to make matters for tragedies, yet could not resist the sweet violence[231] of a tragedy. And if it wrought no further good in him, it was that he, in despite of himself, withdrew himself from hearkening to that which might mollify his hardened heart. But it is not the tragedy they do mislike; for it were too absurd to

---

common to almost all commentators on the genre, but Aristotle was undoubtedly in Sidney's mind as he wrote. The attitude and language of "wounds . . . tissue" suggest Horace, *Epistles*, I, xvi, 40–45, though the association of horror with the exposing of vice was common in the Renaissance rationale for tragedy. See, for example, the prefatory letter to the 1581 edition of *Seneca His Tenne Tragedies*; and Giraldi Cinthio's views (Gilbert, p. 252). The notion that tragedy illustrates and therefore frustrates tyranny was also common; as Elyot puts it (*The Governor*, p. 41): "And whan a man is comen to mature yeres . . . than shall he, in redying tragoedies, execrate and abhorre the intollerable life of tyrantes." The terms "admiration" and "commiseration" are a variation on Aristotle's "pity" and "fear" (*Poetics*, VI), though that they illustrate "the uncertainty of this world" is an addition that derives from the medieval rather than the classical world view. The medieval conception of an arbitrary Fortune, and the related tradition of contempt for the world, which were fused and modified in *A Mirror for Magistrates* (1559), formed the background from which Elizabethan views of tragedy emerged. For further discussion see Smith, I, 392–93; Gilbert, pp. 459–61; Shepherd, pp. 189–90; and Willard Farnham, *The Medieval Heritage of Elizabethan Tragedy* (1936).

[229]"The cruel tyrant who rules with harsh authority fears those who fear him, and fear returns upon its author" (slightly misquoted from Seneca, *Oedipus*, III, 705–6).

[230]Sidney's information on Alexander of Pherae, a tyrant of the fourth century B.C., derives from Plutarch's *Life of Pelopidas*, XXIX. Plutarch records that Alexander, though known to be an immensely cruel person, left a performance of Euripides' *Troades* for fear of being seen weeping.

[231]Gilbert (p. 433) points out that the Greek word for "sweet" (*hadus*) appears several times in Aristotle's discussion of tragedy. However, such oxymorons are a distinguishing characteristic of Sidney's prose.

cast out so excellent a representation of whatsoever is most worthy to be learned.

Is it the lyric[232] that most displeaseth? who with his tuned lyre and well accorded voice giveth praise, the reward of virtue, to virtuous acts; who gives moral precepts and natural problems;[233] who sometimes raiseth up his voice to the height of the heavens in singing the lauds of the immortal God. Certainly, I must confess my own barbarousness, I never heard the old song of Percy and Douglas[234] that I found not my heart moved more than with a trumpet; and yet is it sung but by some blind crowder[235] with no rougher voice than rude style; which, being so evil apparelled in the dust and cobwebs of that uncivil age, what would it work, trimmed in the gorgeous eloquence of Pindar?[236] In Hungary[237] I have seen it the manner at all feasts, and other such meetings, to have songs of their ancestors' valor, which that right soldier-like nation think the chiefest kindlers of brave courage. The incomparable Lacedemonians[238] did not only carry that kind of music ever with them to the field, but even at home, as such songs were made, so were they all content to be the singers of them; when the lusty men were to tell what

[232]With the Greeks the lyric was a song to be sung by an individual performer accompanied by a lyre. Such songs, as Puttenham recognizes (*Arte*, pp. 44–47), could cover a broad range of topics. Sidney is also aware (see pp. 80–81, below) of the more modern conception of the lyric as a brief expression of personal, often amorous, feeling.

[233]"Problems" were questions posed for discussion; a favorite poetic technique, as Ringler points out (*Poems*, p. 460), with the imitators of Petrarch.

[234]Percy and Douglas were antagonists in *The Ballad of Chevy Chase*, a poem probably first composed in the fifteenth century. Percy, the Earl of Northumberland, crosses the Scottish border and meets Douglas. In the battle that follows both leaders are killed.

[235]A fiddler. The crowd is an ancient Welsh stringed instrument.

[236]Pindar (518–438 B.C.), the most celebrated Greek lyric poet, is best remembered for his *Epinicia*, which were written in commemoration of public games.

[237]Sidney visited Hungary in 1573 during his extended continental tour.

[238]The Lacedemonians, or Spartans, were admired for the rigor of their lives and the strict discipline of their military. Plutarch (*Life of Lycurgus*, XXI) describes the Spartans' use of music before and during battles.

they did, the old men what they had done, and the young men what they would do. And where a man may say that Pindar[239] many times praiseth highly victories of small moment, matters rather of sport than virtue; as it may be answered, it was the fault of the poet, and not of the poetry, so indeed the chief fault was in the time and custom of the Greeks, who set those toys at so high a price that Philip of Macedon reckoned a horse-race won at Olympus among his three fearful felicities.[240] But as the unimitable Pindar[241] often did, so is that kind most capable and most fit to awake the thoughts from the sleep of idleness to embrace honorable enterprises.

There rests the heroical,[242] whose very name (I think) should daunt all back-biters; for by what conceit can a tongue be directed to speak evil of that which draweth with it no less champions than Achilles,[243] Cyrus,[244] Aeneas,[245] Turnus,[246] Tydeus,[247] and Rinaldo?[248] who doth not only teach and move to a truth, but teacheth and moveth to the most high and excellent truth; who maketh magnanimity and justice shine throughout all misty fearfulness and foggy desires; who, if the

239See n. 236, above.

240According to Plutarch (*Life of Alexander*, III), Philip of Macedon received news of a victory in battle, a winner at the race track in Olympia, and the birth of Alexander, all on the same day.

241See n. 236, above.

242In spite of Aristotle's preference for tragedy (*Poetics*, XXVI), most Renaissance poets and critics rated epic or heroic poetry as the highest literary form. Although there were a variety of opinions on what the content of heroic poetry should be, it was generally agreed that the genre should take moral instruction as its main objective. This is clear, for example, in Harington's preface to his 1591 translation of *Orlando Furioso* (Smith, II, 198): "What better and more meete studie is there for a young man then Poetrie? specially Heroicall Poesie, that with her sweet statelinesse doth erect the mind & lift it up to the consideration of the highest matters." Cf. also Spenser's letter to Raleigh prefixed to *The Faerie Queene*.

243Achilles appears in Homer's *Iliad*.

244See n. 59, above.

245The hero of Virgil's *Aeneid*.

246See n. 194, above.

247In Statius' *Thebais*, Tydeus appears as one of the Seven against Thebes.

248Rinaldo, a hero in Ariosto's *Orlando Furioso* and Tasso's *Jerusalem Delivered*.

saying of Plato and Tully be true,[249] that who could see virtue would be wonderfully ravished with the love of her beauty, this man sets her out to make her more lovely in her holiday apparel, to the eye of any that will deign not to disdain until they understand. But if anything be already said in the defence of sweet poetry, all concurreth to the maintaining the heroical, which is not only a kind, but the best and most accomplished kind of poetry. For as the image of each action stirreth and instructeth the mind, so the lofty image of such worthies most inflameth the mind with desire to be worthy, and informs with counsel how to be worthy. Only let Aeneas[250] be worn in the tablet of your memory, how he governeth himself in the ruin of his country; in the preserving his old father and carrying away his religious ceremonies;[251] in obeying the god's commandment to leave Dido,[252] though not only all passionate kindness, but even the human consideration of virtuous gratefulness, would have craved other of him; how in storms, how in sports, how in war, how in peace, how a fugitive, how victorious, how besieged, how besieging, how to strangers, how to allies, how to enemies, how to his own; lastly, how in his inward self, and how in his outward government. And, I think, in a mind not prejudiced with a

---

[249]The idea that virtue, if it could be made visible, would rule human lives derives from Plato's *Phaedrus*, 250, though Sidney almost certainly found it translated in Cicero (*De Officiis*, I, v, 15; *De Finibus Bonorum et Malorum*, II, xvi, 52). Like Cicero, Gabriel Harvey was doubtful that virtue could in fact be seen (*Ciceronianus*, ed. Harold S. Wilson and trans. Clarence A. Forbes [1945], p. 99): "If we could only realize in actuality for the public weal what we conceive in mind and imagination for our own delight! But since so few men in all history—if indeed any men at all—have succeeded in really attaining and making manifest what they grasped in contemplation, we can only pray for this as best and best worthy of prayer, but we may not hope for a thing so difficult." But for Sidney, whose esthetic rests on the assumption that poetry makes ideas visible to the mind's eye (see n. 62; n. 65; and n. 118, above), the best literature is replete with images of virtue. The pictorial quality in good poetry, as Sidney argues, not only informs the intellect, but also goads the will into virtuous action. See *Astrophil and Stella*, XXV, and Ringler's note (*Poems*, p. 469).

[250]See n. 245, above.

[251]*Aeneid*, II, 705 ff. By "ceremonies" Sidney means religious objects.

[252]Dido, the queen of Carthage, committed suicide when Aeneas left her. The story appears in *Aeneid*, IV.

pɪₑⱼᵤₐicating humor, he will be found in excellency fruitful; yea, even as Horace saith,

melius Chrysippo et Crantore.[253]

But truly I imagine it falleth out with these poet-whippers, as with some good women, who often are sick, but in faith they cannot tell where. So the name of poetry is odious to them, but neither his cause nor effects, neither the sum that contains him nor the particularities descending from him, give any fast handle to their carping dispraise.

Sith then poetry is of all human learning the most ancient and of most fatherly antiquity, as from whence other learnings have taken their beginnings; sith it is so universal that no learned nation doth despise it, nor no barbarous nation is without it; sith both Roman and Greek gave divine names unto it, the one of prophesying, the other of making, and that indeed, that name of making is fit for him, considering that whereas other arts retain themselves within their subject and receive, as it were, their being from it, the poet only bringeth his own stuff, and doth not learn a conceit out of a matter, but maketh matter for a conceit;[254] sith neither his description nor his end containeth any evil, the thing described cannot be evil; sith his effects be so good as to teach goodness and to delight the learners; sith therein (namely in moral doctrine, the chief of all knowledges) he doth not only far pass the historian, but for instructing is well nigh comparable to the philosopher, and for moving, leaves him behind him; sith the Holy Scripture (wherein there is no uncleanness) hath whole parts in it poetical, and that even our

[253]"Better than Chrysippus and Crantor" (Horace, *Epistles*, I, ii, 4). Horace is explaining to his friend Lollius that Homer is a better teacher of ethics than either Chrysippus or Crantor. Chrysippus (ca. 280–207 B.C.) was an early Stoic, while Crantor (ca. 335–ca. 275 B.C.), according to Cicero (*Tusculan Disputations*, III, vi, 12), ranked among the most eminent Platonists.

[254]The poet does not simply derive his concepts from external nature ("matter"); rather, he generates ideal conceptions in his own mind and then sets them forth in concrete characters and events of his own invention. See n. 55, above.

Saviour Christ vouchsafed to use the flowers of it;[255] sith all his kinds are not only in their united forms, but in their severed dissections, fully commendable; I think (and think I think rightly) the laurel crown appointed for triumphing captains doth worthily (of all other learnings) honor the poet's triumph.[256]

But because we have ears as well as tongues, and that the lightest reasons that may be will seem to weigh greatly if nothing be put in the counter-balance, let us hear, and, as well as we can, ponder, what objections may be made against this art, which may be worthy either of yielding or answering.

First, truly, I note not only in these *mysomousoi*, poet-haters, but in all that kind of people who seek a praise by dispraising others,[257] that they do prodigally spend a great many wandering words in quips and scoffs, carping and taunting at each thing which, by stirring the spleen[258] may stay the brain from a thorough beholding the worthiness of the subject. Those kind of objections, as they are full of very idle easiness, sith there is nothing of so sacred a majesty but that an itching tongue may rub itself upon it, so deserve they no other answer, but instead of laughing at the jest, to laugh at the jester. We know a playing wit can praise the discretion of an ass, the comfortableness of being in debt, and the jolly commodity of being sick of the plague.[259] So of the contrary side, if we will turn Ovid's verse,

Ut lateat virtus proximitate mali,[260]

[255]This is probably a reference to Christ's use of parables in his teaching.

[256]Sidney is perhaps thinking of the crowning of Petrarch (see n. 21, above) as poet laureate at Rome in 1341. In ancient Rome the laurel crown was generally reserved for victorious generals.

[257]For a similar sentiment on selfish and malignant critics, see Daniel, *Musophilus*, ll. 50–61.

[258]Spleen was regarded during the Renaissance as the physiological basis for whimsical or capricious feelings, variously interpreted as the source of laughter, melancholy, or ill temper.

[259]In his discussion of the uses of paradox, or more specifically, ironic praise and dispraise, Sidney has Agrippa and Erasmus (see n. 261 and n. 262, below) as his models.

[260]Adapted from Ovid, *Ars Amatoria*, II, 662. Sidney's Latin and his English translation ("that good lie hid in nearness of the evil") invert

that good lie hid in nearness of the evil, Agrippa[261] will be as
merry in showing the vanity of science as Erasmus[262] was in
commending of folly. Neither shall any man or matter escape
some touch of these smiling railers. But for Erasmus and
Agrippa, they had another foundation than the superficial part
would promise.[263] Marry, these other pleasant fault-finders, who
will correct the verb before they understand the noun, and con-
fute others' knowledge before they confirm their own, I would
have them only remember that scoffing cometh not of wisdom.[264]
So as the best title in true English they get with their merriments
is to be called good fools, for so have our grave forefathers ever
termed that humorous kind of jesters.

But that which giveth greatest scope to their scorning humors
is rhyming and versing. It is already said[265] (and, as I think,
truly said), it is not rhyming and versing that maketh poesy. One
may be a poet without versing, and a versifier without poetry.
But yet presuppose it were inseparable (as indeed it seemeth
Scaliger[266] judgeth), truly it were an inseparable commendation.

Ovid's original: *Et lateat vitium proximitate boni* ("And let its proximity to
a virtue disguise a fault"). For a particularly humorous, if also vicious, application of the Ovidian tag, see Donne's *Elegy II*, "The Anagram."

261Henry Cornelius Agrippa of Nettesheim (1486–1535), a scholar and
occult philosopher, published his skeptical attack on the aspirations of
human reason (*De Incertitudine et Vanitate Scientiarum et Artium*) in
1530. For a typical Elizabethan response, see Harington's *Apology* (Smith,
II, 199–200).

262Erasmus (1466–1536), the famous Dutch humanist, came to England in 1511 to lecture on Greek. His *Moriae Encomium* (translated in
1549 as *Praise of Folly*) was a satirical attack on clerical and theological
abuses.

263Agrippa, in spite of his deep suspicions about the uses of human
reason, and Erasmus, in spite of his paradoxical praising of foolishness, had
the encouragement of piety and simple faith in revealed religion as their
main objectives. On Erasmus, see Walter Kaiser, *Praisers of Folly* (1963),
pp. 17–100.

264"A scorner seeketh wisdom, and findeth it not" (Proverbs 14:6).

265See p. 21 and n. 85, above.

266See Scaliger, *Poetices*, I, 2.

For if *oratio* next to *ratio*, speech next to reason, be the greatest gift bestowed upon mortality,[267] that cannot be praiseless which doth most polish that blessing of speech, which considers each word not only (as a man may say) by his forcible quality,[268] but by his best measured quantity,[269] carrying even in themselves a harmony (without (perchance) number, measure, order, proportion be in our time grown odious). But lay aside the just praise it hath, by being the only fit speech for music[270] (music, I say, the most divine striker of the senses[271]), thus much is undoubtedly true, that if reading be foolish without remembering, memory being the only treasurer of knowledge, those words

[267]This was a commonplace both in the Renaissance and in antiquity. Sidney's view of the relationship between speech and reason may have derived from his reading in Phillipe de Mornay (see n. 63, above, and *Works*, III, 266–68).

[268]Accent.

[269]In classical poetry the basic rhythmic unit is quantitative, based on the time required to pronounce a syllable. English poetry, on the other hand, derives its rhythm from the accent (long or short, stressed or unstressed) given to a syllable. For a short period during the Renaissance, however, there was a controversial and ultimately unsuccessful attempt (centering around Sidney and his associates) to compose English poetry in quantitative meters. Sidney experimented with classical prosody in some of the poems in *Arcadia*, but (happily) his enthusiasm had given way to good sense by the time he began *Astrophil and Stella*. For a full summary of the known details, see Ringler's note (*Poems*, pp. 389–93).

[270]The common Renaissance view that poetry and music are sister arts arose from the observation that both exhibit harmony and rhythm. Puttenham makes numerous comparisons between the two arts, arguing (*Arte*, p. 64) that "Poesie is a skill to speake & write harmonically: and verses or rime be a kind of Musicall utterance, by reason of a certaine congruitie in sounds pleasing the eare." See Neil L. Rudenstine, *Sidney's Poetic Development* (1967), pp. 158–60, 169–71.

[271]As in his later reference to the "planet-like music of poetry" (p. 89), Sidney seems to be alluding to the magical powers traditionally associated with the music of the spheres. In Hoby's translation of *The Courtier* (Everyman ed., p. 75), for example, it is related that "it hath beene the opinion of most wise Philosophers, that the worlde is made of musike, and the heavens in their moving made a melodie, and our soule is framed after the verie same sort and therefore lifteth up it selfe, and (as it were) reviveth the vertues and force of it selfe with Musicke." Cf. Daniel, *Musophilus*, ll. 979–80.

which are fittest for memory are likewise most convenient for knowledge.[272]

Now, that verse far exceedeth prose in the knitting up of the memory, the reason is manifest. The words (besides their delight, which hath a great affinity to memory) being so set as one word cannot be lost but the whole work fails; which accuseth itself, calleth the remembrance back to itself, and so most strongly confirmeth it. Besides, one word so, as it were, begetting another, as be it in rhyme or measured verse, by the former a man shall have a near guess to the follower. Lastly, even they that have taught the art of memory have showed nothing so apt for it as a certain room divided into many places,[273] well and thoroughly known. Now that hath the verse in effect perfectly, every word having his natural seat, which seat must needs make the words remembered. But what needeth more in a thing so known to all men? Who is it that ever was a scholar that doth not carry away some verses of Virgil, Horace, or Cato,[274] which in his youth he learned, and even to his old age serve him for hourly lessons? as

Percontatorem fugito, nam garrulus idem est.[275]

Dum sibi quisque placet, credula turba sumus.[276]

[272]The virtues of poetry as a mnemonic device are obvious enough. During the Renaissance, however, the "art of memory" was a subject of much greater interest and controversy than it is today. Sidney offers his brother some advice on the best techniques for memorization (*Works*, III, 131–32). For a thorough background, see Frances A. Yates, *The Art of Memory* (1966).

[273]One common mnemonic technique was the mental visualization of a room whose various contents could be associated with arguments or relevant facts. The doctrine of "places" (Latin *loci*) held a prominent position in Renaissance logic and rhetoric. The *loci communes*, or "commonplaces," were general headings or categories, often visually conceived, beneath which the details of an argument could be arranged. See Sister Joan Marie Lechner, *Renaissance Concepts of the Commonplaces* (1962).

[274]See n. 74, above.

[275]"Shun the inquisitive man, for he is a talker" (Horace, *Epistles*, I, xviii, 69).

[276]"While each of us pleases himself, we are a credulous crew" (Ovid, *Remedium Amoris*, 686). "as . . . *sumus*" appears neither in Olney nor in Norwich, but is unique to Ponsonby.

But the fitness it hath for memory is notably proved by all delivery of arts:[277] wherein for the most part, from grammar to logic, mathematic, physic, and the rest, the rules chiefly necessary to be borne away are compiled in verses. So that verse, being in itself sweet and orderly, and being best for memory, the only handle of knowledge, it must be in jest that any man can speak against it.

Now then go we to the most important imputations laid to the poor poets.[278] For aught I can yet learn, they are these. First, that there being many other more fruitful knowledges, a man might better spend his time in them than in this.[279] Secondly, that it is the mother of lies.[280] Thirdly, that it is the nurse of abuse,[281] infecting us with many pestilent desires, with a siren's sweetness drawing the mind to the serpent's tail of sinful fancy. And herein especially comedies give the largest field to ear,[282] as Chaucer saith;[283] how both in other nations and in ours, before

[277]The notion that poetry is an aid to the memory, an assumption familiar in and before Sidney's time, resulted in numerous versified handbooks on the various sciences. The Italian medical school at Salerno, for example, was famous for a metrical treatise on the preservation of physical health dedicated to Robert of Normandy. Cf. Puttenham, *Arte*, p. 12; Smith, II, 207; and Daniel, p. 133.

[278]Plato's familiar condemnation of poets (*Republic*, X, 595 ff.), a strong medieval tradition of distrust for imaginative literature, and the moral and social attack from the ranks of the Puritans (see Introduction), all contribute to the background of "important imputations" that Sidney is about to confront. The parties to the controversy are far too numerous to mention; and the issues—springing from the central question of the nature and uses of imitation—are almost as diverse. The eloquent arguments of Sidney's defense were formative in the minds of later Elizabethan commentators. Cf. particularly Harington (Smith, II, 199 ff.) and Daniel (pp. 125–58).

[279]This is the general position of Philocosmus in Daniel's *Musophilus*.

[280]The second imputation, that poetic imitation operates at two removes from the truth, is Plato's. Sidney's rebuttal is implicit in his definition of poetry as an imitation of things not as they are, but as they should be (see pp. 12–15, above).

[281]This is Gosson's position (see Introduction).

[282]To plough. Only Ponsonby has "ear." Both Norwich and Olney read "err."

[283]*The Knight's Tale*, l. 28. Sidney is alluding to the words, but not the sense, of Chaucer's phrase.

poets did soften us, we were full of courage, given to martial exercises, the pillars of manlike liberty, and not lulled asleep in
shady idleness with poets' pastimes.[284] And lastly, and chiefly,
they cry out with an open mouth, as if they had outshot Robin
Hood,[285] that Plato banished them out of his commonwealth.[286]
Truly, this is much, if there be much truth in it.

First, to the first, that a man might better spend his time is a
reason indeed; but it doth (as they say) but *petere principium:*[287]
for if it be, as I affirm, that no learning is so good as that which
teacheth and moveth to virtue, and that none can both teach
and move thereto so much as poetry, then is the conclusion
manifest that ink and paper cannot be to a more profitable purpose employed. And certainly, though a man should grant their
first assumption, it should follow (methinks) very unwillingly,
that good is not good because better is better. But I still and ut-
terly deny that there is sprung out of earth a more fruitful knowledge.

To the second therefore, that they should be the principal
liars, I answer paradoxically, but truly, I think truly, that of all
writers under the sun the poet is the least liar, and, though he
would, as a poet can scarcely be a liar. The astronomer,[288] with
his cousin the geometrician, can hardly escape, when they take
upon them to measure the height of the stars. How often, think

284Musidorus, one of the heroes in *Arcadia*, accuses his friend Pyrocles,
who has abandoned the life of heroic action, of nourishing his idleness
"with the conceites of the poets" (*Works*, I, 58).

285The allusion to Robin Hood, as Harington points out (Smith, II, 219),
is proverbial: "But as our English proverb saith, many talke of Robin Hood
that never shot in his bow."

286*Republic*, X, 595 ff. Gosson (*School*, p. 20) thought it "no marveyle
though Plato shut them out of his Schoole, and banished them quite from
his common wealth, as effeminate writers, unprofitable members, and utter
enemies to vertue."

287"To beg the question."

288A. C. Hamilton ("Sidney and Agrippa," *Review of English Studies*,
VII [1956], 151–57) has pointed out a number of parallels between Sidney
and Agrippa in their treatment of the sciences. On Agrippa, see n. 261,
above.

you, do the physicians lie when they aver things good for sickness, which afterwards send Charon[289] a great number of souls drowned in a potion before they come to his ferry? And no less of the rest, which take upon them to affirm. Now for the poet, he nothing affirms, and therefore never lieth. For, as I take it, to lie is to affirm that to be true which is false; so as the other artists, and especially the historian, affirming many things, can, in the cloudy knowledge of mankind, hardly escape from many lies. But the poet (as I said before) never affirmeth. The poet never maketh any circles about your imagination[290] to conjure you to believe for true what he writes. He citeth not authorities of other histories, but even for his entry calleth the sweet Muses to inspire into him a good invention; in troth, not laboring to tell you what is or is not, but what should or should not be. And therefore, though he recount things not true, yet because he telleth them not for true, he lieth not, without we will say that Nathan[291] lied in his speech before alleged to David; which, as a wicked man durst scarce say, so think I none so simple would say that Aesop[292] lied in the tales of his beasts; for who thinks that Aesop writ it for actually true were well worthy to have his name chronicled among the beasts he writeth of. What child is there that, coming to a play, and seeing Thebes written in great letters upon an old door, doth believe that it is Thebes? If then a man can arrive at that child's age to know that the poet's persons and doings are but pictures what should be,[293] and not stories what have been, they will never give the lie to things not affirmatively but allegorically and figuratively written. And therefore, as in history looking for truth, they go away full

[289]Charon was the ferryman of Greek myth who conveyed the shades of the dead across the rivers of the underworld.

[290]The poet never uses magic to charm his readers into accepting falsehoods. Fulke Greville (*Caelica*, LXXVII, 9) speaks of "Circles to enthrall Mens hearts."

[291]See n. 204, above.

[292]See n. 139, above.

[293]See pp. 12–15, above.

fraught with falsehood, so in poesy looking for fiction, they shall use the narration but as an imaginative ground-plot of a profitable invention.[294]

But hereto is replied that the poets give names to men they write of, which argueth a conceit of an actual truth, and so, not being true, proves a falsehood. And doth the lawyer lie then, when under the names of John a Stile and John a Noakes[295] he puts his case? But that is easily answered. Their naming of men is but to make their picture the more lively, and not to build any history: painting men, they cannot leave men nameless. We see we cannot play at chess but that we must give names to our chessmen; and yet, methinks, he were a very partial champion of truth that would say we lied for giving a piece of wood the reverend title of a Bishop. The poet nameth Cyrus[296] or Aeneas no other way than to show what men of their fames, fortunes, and estates should do.

Their third is, how much it abuseth men's wit, training it to wanton sinfulness and lustful love: for indeed that is the principal, if not the only, abuse I can hear alleged. They say the comedies rather teach than reprehend amorous conceits. They say the lyric is larded with passionate sonnets, the elegiac weeps the want of his mistress, and that even to the heroical Cupid hath ambitiously climbed.[297] Alas, Love, I would thou couldst as

---

[294]The "ground-plot" is a bare skeleton or frame upon which the reader is to work out ("invent") the full meaning of the poet's original "*Idea* or fore-conceit" (see p. 16, above, and n. 62).

[295]These are fictitious names equivalent to our John Doe. Both Ponsonby and Norwich read: "John of the Stile and John of the Noakes."

[296]See n. 59, above.

[297]Cupid's invasion of the world of heroic action is one of the central themes in Sidney's *Arcadia*. In the original version, which was written before the *Apology*, the full range of Love's potential powers is set forth (*Works*, IV, 17): "Love hathe that excellent nature in yt, that yt dothe transforme the very essence of the Lover, into the thinge loved, uniting, and as yt were incorporating yt, with a secrett, and Inward worcking, and herein doo these kyndes of Love imitate ye excellent. For, as the Love of heaven makes one heavenly, the love of vertue vertuous, so dothe the love of the Worlde make one become worldly, and this effeminate love of a Woman, dothe so womanish a man, that, yf yow yeelde to yt, yt will not onely make yow a

well defend thyself as thou canst offend others. I would those on whom thou dost attend could either put thee away, or yield good reason why they keep thee. But grant love of beauty to be a beastly fault (although it be very hard, sith only man, and no beast, hath that gift to discern beauty); grant that lovely name of love to deserve all hateful reproaches (although even some of my masters the philosophers spent a good deal of their lamp-oil in setting forth the excellency of it); grant, I say, whatsoever they will have granted, that not only love, but lust, but vanity, but (if they list) scurrility, possesseth many leaves of the poet's books; yet think I, when this is granted, they will find their sentence may with good manners put the last words foremost, and not say that poetry abuseth man's wit, but that man's wit abuseth poetry.

For I will not deny but that man's wit may make poesy (which should be *eikastike*,[298] which some learned have defined, figuring forth good things) to be *phantastike*,[298] which doth contrariwise infect the fancy with unworthy objects; as the painter, that should give to the eye either some excellent perspective, or some fine picture fit for building or fortification, or containing in it some notable example, as Abraham sacrificing his son Isaac,[299] Judith killing Holofernes,[300] David fighting with Goliath,[301] may leave those, and please an ill-pleased eye with wanton

---

famous Amazon but a Launder, a Distaff spinner, or whatsoever other vyle occupation theyre idle heades can imagyn, and theyre weyke handes performe." See Mark Rose, *Heroic Love* (1968), chs. 1–2.

[298]*Eikastike* ("imitative," the creation of a perfect likeness) and *phantastike* ("fanciful," the creation of a semblance) are terms which appear in Plato's *Sophist*, 235–36. The distinction between likenesses and mere semblances leads to the conclusion that artists and sophists do not create perfect images of things, but deal with fanciful illusions, at two removes from the truth. In Sidney's usage, however, the terms are not used to explain the proximity of images to their models, but to make a moral distinction between "figuring forth good things" and presenting "unworthy objects." Cf. Puttenham, *Arte*, pp. 18–21.

[299]Genesis 22.

[300]This story appears in the thirteenth chapter of the apocryphal book of Judith.

[301]I Samuel 17.

shows of better hidden matters. But what, shall the abuse of a thing make the right use odious? Nay truly, though I yield that poesy may not only be abused, but that being abused, by the reason of his sweet charming force it can do more hurt than any other army of words, yet shall it be so far from concluding that the abuse should give reproach to the abused, that contrariwise it is a good reason that whatsoever being abused doth most harm, being rightly used (and upon the right use each thing conceiveth his title) doth most good.

Do we not see the skill of physic[302] (the best rampire[303] to our often-assaulted bodies), being abused, teach poison the most violent destroyer? Doth not knowledge of law, whose end is to even and right all things, being abused, grow the crooked fosterer of horrible injuries? Doth not (to go to the highest) God's word abused breed heresy, and His name abused become blasphemy? Truly a needle cannot do much hurt, and as truly (with leave of ladies be it spoken) it cannot do much good. With a sword thou mayest kill thy father, and with a sword thou mayest defend thy prince and country. So that, as in their calling poets the fathers of lies[304] they say nothing, so in this their argument of abuse they prove the commendation.

They allege herewith that before poets began to be in price our nation hath set their hearts' delight upon action, and not upon imagination, rather doing things worthy to be written than writing things fit to be done. What that before time was, I think scarcely Sphinx[305] can tell, sith no memory is so ancient that hath the precedence of poetry.[306] And certain it is that, in our plainest homeliness, yet never was the Albion[307] nation without poetry. Marry, this argument, though it be levelled

---

[302]Medicine.

[303]Rampart or fortification.

[304]Gosson uses the identical phrase (*School*, p. 21).

[305]The Sphinx was the monster (half-woman and half-lion) whose riddle was solved by Oedipus.

[306]Sidney has already argued (p. 6, above) that poets were the first historians.

[307]Albion was an ancient name for Britain.

against poetry, yet is it indeed a chain-shot against all learning, or bookishness, as they commonly term it. Of such mind were certain Goths,[308] of whom it is written that, having in the spoil of a famous city taken a fair library, one hangman (belike fit to execute the fruits of their wits) who had murdered a great number of bodies, would have set fire on it. No, said another very gravely, take heed what you do, for while they are busy about these toys, we shall with more leisure conquer their countries. This indeed is the ordinary doctrine of ignorance, and many words sometimes I have heard spent in it; but because this reason is generally against all learning as well as poetry, or rather all learning but[309] poetry; because it were too large a digression to handle, or at least too superfluous (sith it is manifest that all government of action is to be gotten by knowledge, and knowledge best by gathering many knowledges, which is reading[310]), I only, with Horace, to him that is of that opinion,

> *Jubeo stultum esse libenter;*[311]

for as for poetry itself, it is the freest from this objection.

For poetry is the companion of camps.[312] I dare undertake *Orlando Furioso*[313] or honest King Arthur, will never displease a soldier: but the quiddity of *ens* and *prima materia*[314] will hardly agree with a corselet.[315] And therefore, as I said in the

---

[308]The Goths were a German tribe who sacked Athens in A.D. 267. The story appears, as Cook notes (p. 104), in a continuation of Dio Cassius' *Roman Histories*, LIV, 17, and also in Montaigne's essay, *Of Pedantism*.

[309]Except.

[310]Musidorus urges a similar view on his wayward friend Pyrocles in *Arcadia* (*Works*, I, 55).

[311]"I readily bid him to be a fool" (adapted from Horace, *Satires*, I, i, 63).

[312]The education of the princes in *Arcadia* (*Works*, I, 189–90) illustrates this assertion. See Smith, I, 395.

[313]*Orlando Furioso*, Ariosto's heroic poem, was published in complete form in 1532.

[314]Sidney is mocking the elaborate language of scholastic philosophy (see p. 24, above, and n. 100). A "quiddity" is the essence of a thing; *ens* is pure being; and *prima materia* is primary or uninformed matter.

[315]A piece of armor designed to protect the torso.

beginning,[316] even Turks and Tartars are delighted with poets. Homer, a Greek, flourished before Greece flourished. And if to a slight conjecture a conjecture may be opposed, truly it may seem that, as by him their learned men took almost their first light of knowledge, so their active men received their first motions of courage. Only Alexander's example may serve, who by Plutarch is accounted of such virtue that fortune was not his guide,[317] but his foot-stool; whose acts speak for him, though Plutarch did not,[318] indeed the phoenix of warlike princes. This Alexander left his schoolmaster, living Aristotle, behind him, but took dead Homer with him.[319] He put the philosopher Callisthenes[320] to death for his seeming philosophical, indeed mutinous, stubbornness; but the chief thing he ever was heard to wish for was that Homer had been alive. He well found he received more bravery of mind by the pattern of Achilles than by hearing the definition of fortitude. And therefore, if Cato misliked Fulvius for carrying Ennius[321] with him to the field, it may be answered that if Cato misliked it, the noble Fulvius liked it, or else he had not done it: for it was not the excellent Cato Uticensis[322] (whose authority I would much more have reverenced), but it was the

[316]See p. 9, above.

[317]This is a reference to Plutarch, *Moralia* (*On The Fortune or The Virtue of Alexander*), where Alexander's virtues, and not his good fortune, determine the course of events.

[318]Even if Plutarch had not spoken for him.

[319]Plutarch, in his *Life of Alexander*, VII–VIII, relates that Philip of Macedon gave Aristotle a good wage to tutor his son, Alexander. Plutarch adds that Alexander was very fond of Homer's *Iliad*, and considered the book a useful guide to military discipline.

[320]Callisthenes was Aristotle's nephew and Alexander's historian. After a quarrel with Alexander he was accused of conspiracy and executed.

[321]Fulvius, who became the Roman consul in 189 B.C., was accompanied on a military mission by Ennius (239–169 B.C.), the so-called father of Roman poetry. Cato (234–149 B.C.), known as "the Elder" to distinguish him from his great-grandson (see n. 322, below), was notorious for his dislike of Fulvius. Also known as "the Censor," Cato is remembered for his stern opposition to Carthage and his efforts to revive traditional Roman morality. Lodge (Smith, I, 73) refers to Gosson's arguments against poetry as "Catoes judgement."

[322]Cato Uticensis was the great-grandson of Cato the Elder. See n. 172, above.

former,[323] in truth a bitter punisher of faults, but else a man that had never well sacrificed to the Graces.[324] He misliked and cried out upon all Greek learning,[325] and yet, being eighty years old, began to learn it, belike fearing that Pluto understood not Latin. Indeed, the Roman laws allowed no person to be carried to the wars but he that was in the soldier's roll, and therefore, though Cato misliked his unmustered[326] person, he misliked not his work. And if he had, Scipio Nasica,[327] judged by common consent the best Roman, loved him. Both the other Scipio brothers,[328] who had by their virtues no less surnames than of Asia and Afric, so loved him that they caused his body to be buried in their sepulcher. So as Cato, his authority being but against his person, and that answered with so far greater than himself, is herein of no validity.

But now indeed my burden is great; now Plato his name is laid upon me, whom I must confess, of all philosophers I have ever esteemed most worthy of reverence,[329] and with great reason, sith of all philosophers he is the most poetical. Yet if he

[323]Cato the Elder. See n. 321, above.

[324]The three Graces, personifying grace and beauty, are usually described as the daughters of Zeus. Sidney is making reference to Cato's reputed indifference to the fine arts.

[325]Plutarch records Cato's dislike for Greek culture, particularly philosophy (*Life of Cato the Censor*, XXIII), and his decision in later life to study Greek (*Life*, II). The allusion to Pluto is not easily explained. Shepherd's gloss (p. 206) seems plausible, though, with Shakespeare (*Troilus and Cressida*, III, iii, 197), Sidney may be confusing Pluto, the god of the underworld, with Plutus, the god of riches, in an ironic reference to Cato's rather ruthless pursuit of wealth (*Life*, XXI).

[326]Not enlisted in the army.

[327]Scipio Nasica was Roman consul in 191 B.C. His popularity with the Roman Senate is attested to in Livy, *Histories*, XXIX, xiv, 8–9.

[328]Scipio Asiaticus, the Roman consul in 190 B.C., earned his name by a victory in Asia in 189 B.C. His brother, Scipio Africanus (236–184 B.C.), one of the most brilliant Roman generals, received his surname in 201 B.C. as the result of his formidable victories in Africa. William Webbe (Smith, I, 233) praises him for his friendship with Ennius, as does Puttenham (*Arte*, p. 16), who calls Africanus "Prince of the Romaines." Cicero (*Pro Archia Poeta Oratio*, IX, 22) remarks that the effigy of Ennius is thought to be visible in the marble of the Scipios' tomb. Cf. John Rainolds, *Oratio*, p. 58, and Ringler's note, p. 86.

[329]See n. 31, above.

will defile the fountain out of which his flowing streams have
proceeded, let us boldly examine with what reasons he did it.
First, truly a man might maliciously object that Plato, being a
philosopher, was a natural enemy of poets: for indeed, after the
philosophers had picked out of the sweet mysteries of poetry the
right discerning true points of knowledge, they forthwith putting
it in method,[330] and making a school-art of that which the poets
did only teach by a divine delightfulness, beginning to spurn at
their guides like ungrateful prentices, were not content to set up
shops for themselves but sought by all means to discredit their
masters; which, by the force of delight being barred them, the
less they could overthrow them, the more they hated them.
For indeed, they found for Homer seven cities, and strave[331]
who should have him for their citizen;[332] where many cities
banished philosophers as not fit members to live among them.
For only repeating certain of Euripides' verses, many Athenians
had their lives saved of the Syracusans, when the Athenians
themselves thought many philosophers unworthy to live.[333]
Certain poets, as Simonides[334] and Pindar,[335] had so prevailed

[330]For the close association of the word "method" with Ramus (see
n. 5, above) and his school, see Wilbur Samuel Howell, *Logic and Rhetoric
in England, 1500–1700* (1956), p. 263.

[331]Olney reads: "they found for Homer, seven cities strove, who should
have him for their citizen." Ponsonby is essentially the same. But the sense
is clearest in Norwich, which is the basis for the alteration in the present
text.

[332]A tradition stemming from a series of epigrams in the *Greek An-
thology* (XVI, 294–99), and perpetuated by Cicero (*Pro Archia Poeta
Oratio*, VIII, 19), held that seven different cities claimed to be Homer's
birthplace. Cf. John Rainolds, *Oratio*, p. 58, and Ringler's note, p. 87.

[333]In 413 B.C. the Athenians, led by Nicias, were defeated by the Syracusans. Plutarch (*Life of Nicias*, XXIX) reports that many of the Athenians were saved from bondage by their knowledge of Euripides, whose poetry
was in great esteem among their captors. In the same *Life of Nicias*, XXIII,
Plutarch relates the harsh fates of philosophers in Athens.

[334]Simonides (ca. 556–468 B.C.) was one of the earliest Greek lyric poets.
In about 476 B.C. he went to Sicily as the guest of Hieron, the ruler of
Syracuse. Simonides is said to have helped to make peace between Hieron
and his brother Theron. Hieron was generous in his patronage of the arts,
which may help to explain Sidney's partiality.

[335]In 476 B.C Pindar went to Hieron's court in Syracuse, where he wrote
several poems celebrating his host's exploits. See n. 236, above.

with Hiero the First, that of a tyrant they made him a just king, where Plato could do so little with Dionysius,[336] that he himself of a philosopher was made a slave.[337] But who should do thus, I confess, should requite the objections made against poets with like cavillation against philosophers; as likewise one should do that should bid one read *Phaedrus* or *Symposium*[338] in Plato, or the discourse of love in Plutarch,[339] and see whether any poet do authorize abominable filthiness, as they do. Again, a man might ask out of what commonwealth Plato did banish them. In sooth, thence where he himself alloweth community of women.[340] So as belike this banishment grew not for effeminate wantonness, sith little should poetical sonnets be hurtful when a man might have what woman he listed. But I honor philosophical instructions, and bless the wits which bred them, so as they be not abused, which is likewise stretched to poetry.

Saint Paul himself (who yet for the credit of poets allegeth twice two poets, and one of them by the name of prophet)[341] setteth a watchword upon philosophy, indeed upon the abuse; so doth Plato, upon the abuse, not upon poetry. Plato found fault that the poets of his time filled the world with wrong

---

[336]Dionysius succeeded as tyrant of Syracuse in 367 B.C. Plato was summoned to Sicily to try to mold the suspicious Dionysius into an ideal ruler; but the experiment was a complete failure, and Plato made a hasty retreat.

[337]On a disastrous return trip to Dionysius' court several years later Plato was temporarily imprisoned.

[338]Sidney is referring to the alleged homosexuality in these works. Scaliger (*Poetices*, I, 2) makes the same charge.

[339]This is probably an allusion to Plutarch's *Amatorius*, a discussion of erotic love which concludes in favor of heterosexuality.

[340]Socrates (*Republic*, V, 457) explains that the Guardians in the ideal state are to possess wives and children in common.

[341]Paul's clearest reference to poets occurs in his description of God to the Athenians (Acts 17:28): "For in him we live, and move, and have our being; as certain also of your own poets have said." Thomas Lodge (Smith, I, 71) points out that Paul had read Aratus of Cilicia (ca. 315–240 B.C.), whose astronomical poem, *Phaénomena*, was very popular in antiquity, and may be the subject of Paul's allusion. Lodge adds that Paul was also familiar with Epimenides, a poet and prophet of Crete, one of whose verses appears in Titus 1:12. Cook notes (p. 109) that the fourth poet is the dramatist Menander (342–291 B.C.), whose aphorism, "Evil communications corrupt good manners," appears in I Corinthians 15:33.

opinions of the gods, making light tales of that unspotted essence, and therefore would not have the youth depraved with such opinions.[342] Herein may much be said; let this suffice: the poets did not induce such opinions, but did imitate those opinions already induced. For all the Greek stories can well testify that the very religion of that time stood upon many and many-fashioned gods, not taught so by the poets, but followed according to their nature of imitation. Who list may read in Plutarch the discourses of Isis and Osiris,[343] of the cause why oracles ceased, of the divine providence, and see whether the theology of that nation stood not upon such dreams, which the poets indeed superstitiously observed, and truly (sith they had not the light of Christ) did much better in it than the philosophers, who, shaking off superstition, brought in atheism. Plato therefore (whose authority I had much rather justly construe than unjustly resist) meant not in general of poets, in those words of which Julius Scaliger saith, *Qua authoritate barbari quidam atque hispidi abuti velint ad poetas e republica exigendos;*[344] but only meant to drive out those wrong opinions of the Deity (whereof now, without further law, Christianity hath taken away all the hurtful belief), perchance (as he thought) nourished by the then esteemed poets. And a man need go no further than to Plato himself to know his meaning: who, in his dialogue called *Ion,*[345] giveth high and rightly divine commendation to

[342]This objection appears in *Republic,* II, 377, where it is argued that children derive their religious conceptions from poets like Homer and Hesiod who describe the gods as immoral.

[343]The topics that Sidney mentions derive from chapters in Plutarch's *Moralia.* The Egyptian deities Osiris and his wife Isis, for example, appear in *De Iside et Osiride.*

[344]"Whose authority some barbarous and insensitive men wish to misuse in order to expel the poets from the state" (*Poetices,* I, 2). Scaliger is discussing the arguments against poets in Plato's *Republic.* Olney leaves out the *e* between *poetas* and *republica* in his text, but corrects the error in his *errata.*

[345]*Ion* is a dialogue in which Socrates outlines the doctrine of divine inspiration, a theory which prescribes that the gods use certain poets as vehicles for their own divine utterances. As Puttenham puts it (*Arte,* p. 3): "And this science [of poetry] in his perfection, can not grow, but by some

poetry. So as Plato, banishing the abuse, not the thing, not banishing it, but giving due honor unto it, shall be our patron and not our adversary. For indeed, I had much rather (sith truly I may do it) show their mistaking of Plato (under whose lion's skin they would make an ass-like braying against poesy) than go about to overthrow his authority; whom, the wiser a man is, the more just cause he shall find to have in admiration; especially sith he attributeth unto poesy more than myself do, namely, to be a very inspiring of a divine force, far above man's wit, as in the afore-named dialogue[346] is apparent.

Of the other side, who would show the honors have been by the best sort of judgments granted them, a whole sea of examples would present themselves: Alexanders, Caesars, Scipios,[347] all favorers of poets; Laelius,[348] called the Roman Socrates, himself a poet, so as part of *Heautontimorumenos* in Terence was supposed to be made by him. And even the Greek Socrates,[349] whom Apollo confirmed to be the only wise man, is said to have spent part of his old time in putting Aesop's fables into verses. And therefore full evil should it become his scholar Plato to put such words in his master's mouth against poets. But what need

---

divine instinct, the Platonicks call it *furor.*" Such an esthetic is obviously inconsistent with Sidney's ideas on imitation, but it provides him with a handle for defending Plato.

[346]Sidney is referring to *Ion* (see n. 345, above). In his conclusion that Plato did not banish the poets from the state, Sidney is certainly wrong. He may be making the most of a difficult problem, or, as Gilbert suggests (p. 445), he may be misinformed. For a modern treatment of the question, see Eric A. Havelock, *Preface to Plato* (1963).

[347]See n. 319 and n. 328, above. Several of the Caesars were interested in poetry, though the example of Augustus Caesar's patronage of Virgil is perhaps most familiar.

[348]Cicero (*De Officiis*, I, xxvi, 90) compares Laelius (born ca. 186 B.C.) to Socrates, and in the same treatise (II, xi, 40) relates that he was given the surname *Sapiens* ("the Wise"), no doubt for his learning and eloquence. Roger Ascham (Smith, I, 28) points out that Laelius had a hand in Terence's *Heautontimorumenos* (*The Self-Tormentor*), and gives Cicero (*Epistulae ad Atticum*, VII, iii, 10) as his source.

[349]The story that the Delphic Oracle pronounced Socrates the wisest of all men appears in Plato's *Apology*, 21. In the *Phaedo*, 60–61, Socrates tells a friend that he is putting the fables of Aesop into verse because of a recurrent dream that urges him to compose.

more? Aristotle writes the Art of Poesy; and why, if it should
not be written? Plutarch teacheth[350] the use to be gathered of
them, and how if they should not be read? And who reads
Plutarch's either history or philosophy, shall find he trimmeth
both their garments with guards of poesy.[351] But I list not to defend poesy with the help of her underling historiography. Let
it suffice[352] that it is a fit soil for praise to dwell upon; and what
dispraise may set upon it, is either easily overcome, or trans-
formed into just commendation.

So that, sith the excellencies of it may be so easily and so
justly confirmed, and the low-creeping objections so soon trodden
down, it not being an art of lies, but of true doctrine; not of
effeminateness, but of notable stirring of courage; not of abusing
man's wit, but of strengthening man's wit; not banished, but
honored by Plato; let us rather plant more laurels for to engar-
land our poets' heads (which honor of being laureate,[353] as
besides them only triumphant captains wear, is a sufficient authority to show the price they ought to be had in), than suffer
the ill-favoring breath of such wrong-speakers once to blow upon
the clear springs of poesy.

But sith I have run so long a career in this matter, methinks
before I give my pen a full stop it shall be but a little more lost
time to inquire why England (the mother of excellent minds)
should be grown so hard a step-mother to poets, who certainly
in wit ought to pass all other, sith all only proceedeth from their
wit, being indeed makers of themselves, not takers of others.
How can I but exclaim

> *Musa, mihi causas memora, quo numine laeso?*[354]

Sweet poesy, that hath anciently had kings, emperors, sena-

350In the *Moralia, How to Study Poetry.*
351Citations from various poets.
352Both Ponsonby and Norwich read "suffice to have showed."
353See n. 256, above.
354"O Muse, remind me of the causes, what deity has been offended"
(*Aeneid*, I, 8). Sidney is using the line in his own context, asking what the
causes are for the present state of poetry in England.

tors, great captains, such as, besides a thousand others, David,[355] Adrian,[356] Sophocles,[357] Germanicus,[358] not only to favor poets, but to be poets. And of our nearer times can present for her patrons a Robert, king of Sicily,[359] the great King Francis of France,[360] King James of Scotland;[361] such cardinals as Bembus[362] and Bibbiena;[363] such famous preachers and teachers as Beza[364] and Melanchthon;[365] so learned philosophers as Fracastorius[366] and Scaliger;[367] so great orators as Pontanus[368] and

[355]See n. 45, above.

[356]Adrian, or Hadrian, Roman Emperor from 117 to 138, was famous for his patronage of art and learning.

[357]Sophocles (495–406 B.C.) was one of the major Greek tragedians.

[358]Germanicus (15 B.C.–A.D. 19), the adopted son of Tiberius, was extremely popular with the Roman people before his early death. In addition to translating, Germanicus did some writing of his own, most of which has been lost.

[359]Robert II of Anjou (1275–1343) was famous in Europe for his love of the arts, and for his patronage of Petrarch.

[360]Francis I (1494–1547), the contemporary and in many ways the personal counterpart of Henry VIII, was instrumental in the development of French culture.

[361]Ringler (*Poems*, xlix) suggests that Sidney is referring to James VI of Scotland, later James I of England (1603–1625). However, it is also possible that Sidney was thinking of James I of Scotland (1394–1437), who is said to have written *The Kingis Quair* while a prisoner in England. Cf. Smith, I, 396; and Shepherd, p. 212.

[362]Pietro Bembo (1470–1547), a cardinal, wrote in both Latin and Italian. He is one of the major characters in Castiglione's *The Courtier*.

[363]Bernardo Dovizi (1470–1520), the "pleasurable Cardinall Bibiena," as Harvey calls him (Smith, I, 125), was celebrated for the humor of his *Calandria*, a comedy whose plot derives from Plautus.

[364]Théodore de Bèze (1519–1605) was the most influential of Calvin's associates, and the leader of the Calvinists in Geneva after Calvin's death in 1564. In 1577 Arthur Golding published *A Tragedie of Abrahams Sacrifice*, a translation from Bèze's original.

[365]Philip Melanchthon (1497–1560) was a German humanist and, after Luther, the most important advocate of religious reform in Germany.

[366]Girolamo Fracastoro (ca. 1483–1553), a poet and philosopher, studied under Pomponazzi at Padua. His Latin poem *Syphilis* was famous in its time; and Sidney may have known his *Naugerius*. See n. 82, above.

[367]Julius Caesar Scaliger (1484–1558), the sometime antagonist of Erasmus, wrote several scientific treatises. His posthumous *Poetices Libri Septem* seems to have been an important book in Sidney's critical background. Cf. Weinberg, II, 743–50.

[368]See n. 78, above.

Muretus;[369] so piercing wits as George Buchanan;[370] so grave counselors as, besides many, but before all, that Hospital of France,[371] than whom (I think) that realm never brought forth a more accomplished judgment, more firmly builded upon virtue—I say these, with numbers of others, not only to read others' poesies, but to poetise for others' reading—that poesy, thus embraced in all other places, should only find in our time a hard welcome in England, I think the very earth lamenteth it, and therefore decketh our soil with fewer laurels than it was accustomed. For heretofore poets have in England also flourished, and, which is to be noted, even in those times when the trumpet of Mars did sound loudest. And now that an over-faint quietness should seem to strew the house for poets, they are almost in as good reputation as the mountebanks at Venice.[372] Truly even that, as of the one side it giveth great praise to poesy, which like Venus (but to better purpose) had rather be troubled in the net with Mars than enjoy the homely quiet of

---

[369]Marc-Antoine Muret (1526–1585) was a French humanist and pedagogue. Convicted of heresy and sodomy at the age of 28, Muret fled to Italy where he converted to Roman Catholicism. See "Muret and the History of 'Attic Prose,' " in Morris Croll, *Style, Rhetoric, and Rhythm* (1966), pp. 107–62.

[370]George Buchanan (1506–1582) was a humanist scholar who, though born in Scotland, spent much of his life in France. For several years (1570–1578) he was tutor to James VI of Scotland. In addition to a major history of Scotland, and *De Jure Regni apud Scotos* (1578), an influential political treatise, Buchanan wrote *De Sphaera*, a Latin didactic poem defending the Ptolemaic system of the universe. Gabriel Harvey (Smith, II, 234) makes note of "the sweete Psalmes of King David, royally translated by Buchanan." See J. E. Phillips, "George Buchanan and the Sidney Circle," *Huntington Library Quarterly*, XII (1948), 23–55.

[371]Lawyer, humanist, poet, and an advocate of religious toleration, Michel de l'Hôpital was Chancellor of France for several years (1560–68).

[372]A mountebank (literally "mount-on-bench") was an Italian variety of the quack doctor who regaled his audience with tricks and jests before peddling his medicines. In Ben Jonson's *Volpone*, which is situated in Venice, the dupe, Sir Politick Would-Be, describes the mountebanks as "the only knowing men of Europe" (II, ii, 9). In the same scene the treacherous Volpone impersonates a mountebank.

Vulcan;[373] so serves it for a piece of a reason why they are less grateful to idle England, which now can scarce endure the pain of a pen. Upon this necessarily followeth that base men with servile wits undertake it, who think it enough if they can be rewarded of the printer. And so as Epaminondas[374] is said, with the honor of his virtue to have made an office, by his exercising it which before was contemptible, to become highly respected; so these, no more but setting their names to it, by their own disgracefulness disgrace the most graceful poesy. For now, as if all the Muses were got with child to bring forth bastard poets, without any commission they do post over the banks of Helicon,[375] till they make the readers more weary than post-horses; while in the meantime they,

> *Queis meliore luto finxit praecordia Titan,*[376]

are better content to suppress the out-flowing of their wit than, by publishing them, to be accounted knights of the same order.[377]

But I, that before ever I durst aspire unto the dignity, am admitted into the company of the paper-blurrers, do find the

---

[373]Vulcan captured his adulterous wife, Venus, and her lover, Mars, in a fine net which he laid over their bed. This originally Homeric story was probably best known to Sidney in Ovid's *Metamorphoses*, IV, 167–89.

[374]Epaminondas (died 362 B.C.) was a Theban general whose military exploits helped to destroy the Spartan supremacy in Greece. Plutarch wrote a *Life of Epaminondas* (now lost), preserved some of his aphorisms (*Moralia, Sayings of Kings and Commanders*, 192–94), and recorded the story that he brought dignity to the task of collecting refuse (*Moralia, Precepts of Statecraft*, 811).

[375]Helicon is the largest mountain in Boeotia, and was once the location of a sanctuary of the Muses. Sidney is making the common error of mistaking the mountain for the spring Hippocrene, a source of poetic inspiration, which was said to have been struck in a rock by the hoof of Pegasus.

[376]"Whose heart Titan has fashioned with finer earth" (adapted from Juvenal, *Satires*, XIV, 35).

[377]Sidney means that poets of quality are reluctant to publish their work for fear of being associated with the "bastard poets."

very true cause of our wanting estimation is want of desert, taking upon us to be poets in despite of Pallas.[378] Now wherein
we want desert were a thank-worthy labor to express; but if I
knew, I should have mended myself. But I, as I never desired
the title, so have I neglected the means to come by it. Only,
over-mastered by some thoughts, I yielded an inky tribute unto
them.[379] Marry, they that delight in poesy itself should seek to
know what they do, and how they do, and especially look themselves in an unflattering glass of reason, if they be inclinable
unto it. For poesy must not be drawn by the ears; it must be
gently led, or rather it must lead; which was partly the cause
that made the ancient-learned affirm it was a divine gift,[380] and
no human skill; sith all other knowledges lie ready for any that
hath strength of wit; a poet no industry can make, if his own
genius be not carried unto it; and therefore is it an old proverb,
orator fit, poeta nascitur.[381] Yet confess I always that as the
fertilest ground must be manured, so must the highest flying
wit have a Daedalus[382] to guide him. That Daedalus, they say,
both in this and in other, hath three wings to bear itself up into
the air of due commendation: that is, Art, Imitation, and Exercise. But these, neither artificial rules[383] nor imitative patterns,[384]
we much cumber ourselves withal. Exercise indeed we do, but
that very fore-backwardly: for where we should exercise to know,
we exercise as having known; and so is our brain delivered of
much matter which never was begotten by knowledge.[385] For

[378]Without wisdom. Pallas Athena was thought to be the personification
of Wisdom.

[379]This is perhaps a reference to *Arcadia*, the first version of which was
near completion by 1580.

[380]This is a reference to the Platonic notion that poetry is the product
of divine inspiration. See n. 345, above.

[381]"The orator is made, the poet born" (a tag of uncertain origin).

[382]Daedalus was a mythical character whose name means "cunning
craftsman." He is remembered for his devotion to the art of sculpture, and
for the unhappy death of his son, Icarus, whose wax wings melted when he
flew too near the sun.

[383]The laws that define a discipline or art.

[384]The things imitated in any art.

[385]As Bacon was to do at greater length, Sidney is impugning the kinds

there being two principal parts, matter to be expressed by words, and words to express the matter; in neither we use Art or Imitation rightly. Our matter is *quodlibet*[386] indeed, though wrongly performing Ovid's verse,

Quicquid conabor dicere, versus erit:[387]

never marshalling it into an assured rank, that almost the readers cannot tell where to find themselves.[388]

Chaucer undoubtedly did excellently in his *Troilus and Criseyde*,[389] of whom truly I know not whether to marvel more, either that he in that misty time could see so clearly, or that we in this clear age walk so stumblingly after him. Yet had he great wants, fit to be forgiven in so reverent antiquity. I account the *Mirror of Magistrates*[390] meetly furnished of beautiful parts, and in the Earl of Surrey's lyrics[391] many things tasting of a noble

---

of intellectual method which result in false knowledge. To paraphrase: We engage in various disciplines, but we do it backwards: for where we would like to know about things as they are in themselves, we commence in our inquiry with assumptions that prejudice our conclusions; and so, as a result of the deficiencies of our method, much of what we think we know is false.

[386]Literally, "what it pleases"; any philosophical or theological question proposed for an exercise in disputation. The term is generally associated with scholastic philosophy.

[387]"Whatever I try to say will turn into verse" (adapted from Ovid's *Tristia*, IV, x, 26).

[388]Sidney continues in his argument that good poetry is necessarily well organized and logically consistent. He finds these qualities lacking in most English poetry.

[389]Chaucer's major narrative poem was admired during the Renaissance for its grave meter, its serious religious conclusion, and the learning that it reflected. Cf. Puttenham, *Arte*, p. 61. Sidney is apparently impressed with the way Chaucer organized his story.

[390]First published in 1559, *A Mirror for Magistrates* is a collection of stories in which illustrious men relate their own downfalls. In 1563 an expanded version appeared, which included Thomas Sackville's justly famous "Induction." See n. 228, above.

[391]Henry Howard, Earl of Surrey (ca. 1517–1547), is remembered for the smooth finish of his poetry, and for his imitation of Italian models. Forty of his poems were published posthumously in a collection popularly known as *Tottel's Miscellany* (1557).

birth, and worthy of a noble mind. *The Shepherd's Calendar* [392] hath much poetry in his eclogues, indeed worthy the reading if I be not deceived. That same framing of his style to an old rustic language I dare not allow,[393] sith neither Theocritus[394] in Greek, Virgil[395] in Latin, nor Sannazzaro[396] in Italian, did affect it. Besides these, do I not remember to have seen but few (to speak boldly) printed that have poetical sinews in them: for proof whereof, let but most of the verses be put in prose, and then ask the meaning, and it will be found that one verse did but beget another, without ordering at the first what should be at the last; which becomes a confused mass of words with a tingling sound of rhyme, barely accompanied with reason.[397]

Our tragedies and comedies (not without cause cried out against), observing rules neither of honest civility nor of skillful poetry, excepting *Gorboduc*[398] (again I say, of those that I have

[392]The first flower of Spenser's poetic genius, and perhaps of Elizabethan poetry, *The Shepherd's Calendar* (1579) was dedicated to Sidney.

[393]In a letter prefixed to *The Shepherd's Calendar*, E.K. speculates on Spenser's reasons for using archaic words in his eclogues. "But whether he useth them by such casualty and custom, or of set purpose and choice, as thinking them fittest for such rustical rudeness of shepherds, either for that their rough sound would make his rhymes more ragged and rustical, or else because such old and obsolete words are most used of country folk, sure I think, and think I think not amiss, that they bring great grace, and, as one would say, authority to the verse."

[394]See n. 211, above.

[395]See n. 211, above.

[396]See n. 208, above.

[397]Sidney's emphatic distinction between "words" and "reason," between the conceptual "inside" of a poem and the language on the "outside," is in conformity with the habits of his age. It was standard in Renaissance logic and rhetoric (see n. 53, above) to treat "invention" and "disposition," the discovery and formulation of ideas, in separation from elocution, the application of language to concepts. Such a sense of the division between words and thoughts underlies Sidney's assurance that a good poem will be logically consistent when reduced to prose.

[398]*Gorboduc*, first performed in 1562, was among the earliest English tragedies. Thomas Norton (1532–1584) wrote the first three acts, and Thomas Sackville (see n. 390, above) the last two. The play had its model in the tragedies of Seneca (ca. 4 B.C.–A.D. 65), whose elaborately rhetorical manner and preoccupation with death and revenge had a profound influence on the development of English drama.

seen), which notwithstanding, as it is full of stately speeches and well sounding phrases, climbing to the height of Seneca his style,[399] and as full of notable morality, which it doth most delightfully teach, and so obtain the very end of poesy; yet in troth it is very defectious in the circumstances, which grieveth me, because it might not remain as an exact model of all tragedies. For it is faulty both in place and time,[400] the two necessary companions of all corporal actions. For where the stage should always represent but one place, and the uttermost time presupposed in it should be, both by Aristotle's precept and common reason, but one day, there is both many days and many places inartificially[401] imagined.

But if it be so in *Gorboduc*, how much more in all the rest? where you shall have Asia of the one side, and Afric of the other, and so many other under-kingdoms, that the player, when he cometh in, must ever begin with telling where he is, or else the tale will not be conceived. Now ye shall have three ladies walk to gather flowers, and then we must believe the stage to be a garden. By and by we hear news of shipwreck in the same place, and then we are to blame if we accept it not for a rock. Upon the back of that comes out a hideous monster with fire

[399]Note the pun on "style."
In its most familiar form the English Senecan tradition is associated with the bombastic rhetoric and complex plotting of plays like Thomas Kyd's *The Spanish Tragedy*. But a less popular, less sensational line of Senecan influence began to emerge in the 1590s under the patronage of Sidney's sister, the Countess of Pembroke. Plays such as Samuel Daniel's *Cleopatra* and Fulke Greville's *Mustapha* illustrate the kind of neo-classical Senecanism, with its emphasis on "stately speeches" and "notable morality," that Sidney had in mind when he wrote his *Apology*.

[400]The unities of place and time have a much slighter classical precedent than the unity of action or plot. Aristotle (*Poetics*, VIII) stresses the importance of the causal relations between the parts of a plot. Unity of time—the notion that a tragedy should confine itself to a single revolution of the sun—is also Aristotelian (*Poetics*, V), though Renaissance critics adhered to the precept more dogmatically than was intended. The unity of place has no source in antiquity, but was first formulated by Lodovico Castelvetro in 1571 (see Gilbert, p. 354).

[401]Artlessly.

and smoke, and then the miserable beholders are bound to take
it for a cave. While in the meantime two armies fly in, represented with four swords and bucklers, and then what hard heart
will not receive it for a pitched field?

Now of time they are much more liberal, for ordinary it is
that two young princes fall in love. After many traverses, she is
got with child, delivered of a fair boy, he is lost, groweth a man,
falls in love, and is ready to get another child, and all this in two
hours' space: which, how absurd it is in sense, even sense may
imagine, and art hath taught, and all ancient examples justified,
and at this day, the ordinary players in Italy will not err in. Yet
will some bring in an example of *Eunuchus* in Terence,[402] that
containeth matter of two days, yet far short of twenty years.
True it is, and so was it to be played in two days, and so fitted
to the time it set forth. And though Plautus hath in one place
done amiss,[403] let us hit with him, and not miss with him. But
they will say, how then shall we set forth a story which containeth both many places and many times? And do they not
know that a tragedy is tied to the laws of poesy, and not of history,[404] not bound to follow the story, but having liberty, either
to feign a quite new matter, or to frame the history to the most
tragical conveniency? Again, many things may be told which
cannot be showed, if they know the difference betwixt reporting
and representing. As for example, I may speak (though I am
here) of Peru, and in speech digress from that to the description
of Calicut; but in action I cannot represent it without Pacolet's
horse.[405] And so was the manner the ancients took, by some

402Sidney's reference to Terence's *Eunuch* is probably an error, for the
action of the play occurs in a single day. Cook (pp. 119–20) points out that
Sidney may be confusing the *Eunuch* with *The Self-Tormentor*, where the
action takes more than one day.

403Perhaps, as Shepherd suggests (p. 221), this is an allusion to Plautus'
Captives, which Scaliger (*Poetices*, VI, 3) criticizes for its improbability.

404Aristotle (*Poetics*, IX) argues that the poet need not relate things as
they actually happened (which is the task of the historian), but merely
what might happen. The topic was much discussed by Renaissance critics.

405Pacolet is a dwarf in a French romance which appeared in England
(ca. 1550) as *Valentine and Orson*. Pacolet has a fabulous horse which
transports him instantly wherever he wishes to go.

nuncius[406] to recount things done in former time or other place.

Lastly, if they will represent an history, they must not (as Horace saith) begin *ab ovo*,[407] but they must come to the principal point of that one action which they will represent. By example this will be best expressed. I have a story[408] of young Polydorus, delivered for safety's sake, with great riches, by his father Priam, to Polymnestor, king of Thrace, in the Trojan war time. He, after some years, hearing the overthrow of Priam, for to make the treasure his own, murdereth the child. The body of the child is taken up by Hecuba. She, the same day, findeth a sleight to be revenged most cruelly of the tyrant. Where now would one of our tragedy writers begin, but with the delivery of the child? Then should he sail over into Thrace, and so spend I know not how many years, and travel numbers of places. But where doth Euripides? Even with the finding of the body, leaving the rest to be told by the spirit of Polydorus. This need no further to be enlarged; the dullest wit may conceive it.

But besides these gross absurdities, how all their plays be neither right tragedies, nor right comedies, mingling kings and clowns not because the matter so carrieth it, but thrust in clowns by head and shoulders, to play a part in majestical matters, with neither decency nor discretion, so as neither the admiration and commiseration,[409] nor the right sportfulness,[410] is by their mongrel tragi-comedy[411] obtained. I know Apuleius[412] did somewhat

---

[406]"Messenger." Most Renaissance critics thought of the role of the messenger as a device for reporting horrible events without actually portraying them on stage. Sidney may be following Castelvetro (see Gilbert, pp. 309–10).

[407]"From the egg" (Horace, *Ars Poetica*, 147).

[408]Sidney is about to outline the plot of Euripides' *Hecuba*.

[409]See n. 228, above.

[410]The end of comedy.

[411]Tragi-comedy is a term usually applied to the type of play developed by Beaumont and Fletcher in the first decade of the seventeenth century. Fletcher, in his preface to *The Faithful Shepherdess* (ca. 1610), states that "A tragie-comedie is not so called in respect of mirth and killing, but in respect it wants deaths, which is inough to make it no tragedie, yet brings some neere it, which is inough to make it no comedie."

[412]Apuleius (born ca. A.D. 123) was a Latin poet and philosopher whose most famous work, *Metamorphoses* (best known as *The Golden Ass*),

so, but that is a thing recounted with space of time, not represented in one moment: and I know the ancients have one or two examples of tragi-comedies, as Plautus hath *Amphitrio*.[413] But if we mark them well, we shall find that they never, or very daintily, match horn-pipes and funerals. So falleth it out, that having indeed no right comedy, in that comical part of our tragedy we have nothing but scurrility, unworthy of any chaste ears, or some extreme show of doltishness, indeed fit to lift up a loud laughter, and nothing else: where the whole tract of a comedy should be full of delight, as the tragedy should be still maintained in a well raised admiration.

But our comedians think there is no delight without laughter;[414] which is very wrong, for though laughter may come with delight, yet cometh it not of delight, as though delight should be the cause of laughter; but well may one thing breed both together: nay, rather in themselves they have, as it were, a kind of contrariety; for delight we scarcely do, but in things that have a conveniency to ourselves, or to the general nature; laughter almost ever cometh of things most disproportioned to ourselves and nature. Delight hath a joy in it, either permanent or present. Laughter hath only a scornful tickling. For example, we are ravished with delight to see a fair woman, and yet are far from

---

exhibits a mingling of genres. Sidney allows for the mixture in *The Golden Ass*, just as he does in his own *Arcadia*, because the pastoral episodes in each work are integrated into a unified narrative. See Kenneth Orne Myrick, *Sir Philip Sidney as a Literary Craftsman* (1935), p. 119.

[413]Scaliger remarks (*Poetices*, I, 7) that Plautus thought of his *Amphitryon* as a mixture of tragic and comic qualities.

[414]Sidney's distinction between laughter and delight is clearly illustrated in his own works. Delight (see n. 180, above) is the poet's power of sustaining the interest of his audience. Strictly speaking, delight is not an intellectual apprehension of truth, but an intuitive assent to what is naturally good or beautiful. In *Astrophil and Stella*, "Seventh song," for example, delight is "ravishing" (*Poems*, p. 217); and in *Arcadia* (*Works*, I, 169) Philoclea responds with instinctive delight to the disguised Pyrocles. Laughter, on the other hand, is the appropriate reaction to what is deformed or unnatural. Trissino (see Gilbert, pp. 227–28) says as much. Most of the low characters in *Arcadia* are designed to elicit laughter, but none of them have any claim on our delight (see n. 225, above). See Shepherd, pp. 223–25.

being moved to laughter. We laugh at deformed creatures, wherein certainly we cannot delight. We delight in good chances, we laugh at mischances; we delight to hear the happiness of our friends or country, at which he were worthy to be laughed at that would laugh; we shall contrarily laugh sometimes to find a matter quite mistaken and go down the hill against the bias,[415] in the mouth of some such men, as for the respect of them one shall be heartily sorry, yet he cannot choose but laugh; and so is rather pained than delighted with laughter. Yet deny I not but that they may go well together; for as in Alexander's picture[416] well set out, we delight without laughter, and in twenty mad antics we laugh without delight, so in Hercules,[417] painted with his great beard and furious countenance, in a woman's attire, spinning at Omphale's commandment, it breedeth both delight and laughter. For the representing of so strange a power in love procureth delight, and the scornfulness of the action stirreth laughter.

But I speak to this purpose, that all the end of the comical part be not upon such scornful matters as stirreth laughter only, but, mixed with it, that delightful teaching which is the end of poesy. And the great fault even in that point of laughter, and forbidden plainly by Aristotle,[418] is that they stir laughter in sinful things, which are rather execrable than ridiculous: or in miserable, which are rather to be pitied than scorned. For what is it to make folks gape at a wretched beggar or a beggarly clown;

[415]This is an allusion to the game of bowls. The balls used in bowls are not perfectly round, but have a bias which causes them to curve as they roll.

[416]Plutarch, in his *Life of Alexander*, IV, discusses Apelles' famous painting of Alexander.

[417]Hercules, the legendary hero of Greece and Rome, is said to have performed humiliating and effeminate tasks for Omphale, the queen of Lydia. Pyrocles, one of the Arcadian princes, having disguised himself as an Amazon in order to gain access to his mistress, secures his/her cape "with a very riche jewell: the devise wherof (as he after saw) was this: a *Hercules* made in little fourme, but a distaffe set within his hand as he once was by Omphales commaundement with a worde in Greeke, but thus to be interpreted, *Never more valiant*" (*Works*, I, 75–76).

[418]*Poetics*, V; and *Nicomachean Ethics*, IV, 8.

or against law of hospitality, to jest at strangers because they speak not English so well as we do? What do we learn? sith it is certain

> *Nil habet infelix paupertas durius in se,*
> *Quam quod ridiculos homines facit.*[419]

But rather a busy loving courtier; a heartless threatening Thraso;[420] a self-wise-seeming schoolmaster;[421] an awry-transformed traveler: these, if we saw walk in stage names, which we play naturally, therein were delightful laughter, and teaching delightfulness: as in the other, the tragedies of Buchanan[422] do justly bring forth a divine admiration. But I have lavished out too many words of this play matter. I do it because, as they are excelling parts of poesy, so is there none so much used in England, and none can be more pitifully abused; which, like an unmannerly daughter, showing a bad education, causeth her mother poesy's honesty to be called in question.

Other sorts of poetry almost have we none, but that lyrical kind of songs and sonnets: which, Lord, if He gave us so good minds, how well it might be employed, and with how heavenly fruit, both private and public, in singing the praises of the immortal beauty,[423] the immortal goodness of that God who giveth us hands to write and wits to conceive; of which we might well want words, but never matter; of which we could turn our eyes to nothing but we should ever have new budding occasions. But

---

[419]"Luckless poverty involves nothing more regrettable than that it makes men ridiculous" (Juvenal, *Satires*, III, 152–53).

[420]See n. 224, above.

[421]Rombus, the vain pedant in Sidney's *The Lady of May* (*Works*, II, 208–17), certainly fits this description.

[422]Sidney is probably thinking of Buchanan's *Jephthes* and *Baptistes*. See n. 370, above.

[423]Sidney is setting forth the conventional neo-Platonic theory of love, which prescribes that the mistress reflects higher forms, and is thus the vehicle through which the poet contemplates the ideal. In *Astrophil and Stella*, III (*Poems*, p. 166), for example, Astrophil argues:
> in *Stella*'s face I reed,
> What Love and Beautie be, then all my deed
> But copying is, what in her Nature writes.

truly many of such writings as come under the banner of unresistable love,[424] if I were a mistress, would never persuade me they were in love; so coldly they apply fiery speeches, as men that had rather read lovers' writings, and so caught up certain swelling phrases,[425] which hang together, like a man which once told me the wind was at north-west and by south, because he would be sure to name winds enough, than that in truth they feel these passions, which easily (as I think) may be bewrayed by that same forcibleness or *energia*[426] (as the Greeks call it) of the writer. But let this be a sufficient though short note, that we miss the right use of the material point of poesy.

Now, for the outside of it, which is words, or (as I may term it) diction, it is even well worse. So is that honey-flowing matron eloquence apparelled, or rather disguised, in a courtesan-like painted affectation: one time with so far fet words, that may seem monsters, but must seem strangers to any poor Englishman;[427] another time, with coursing of a letter, as if they were bound to follow the method of a dictionary;[428] another time, with figures and flowers, extremely winter-starved. But I would this fault

[424]Cf. The Song of Solomon 2:4.

[425]In *Astrophil and Stella*, VI (*Poems*, pp. 167–68), Astrophil criticizes those who simply imitate the "swelling phrases" of other poets, and then asserts that his own poems are not copies, but the expression of personal feeling.

[426]*Energia* is a very specific kind of "energy." Aristotle (*Rhetoric*, III, 10 ff.) and Scaliger (*Poetices*, III, 26) both emphasize that *energia* (*efficacia* in Scaliger) is that quality in language which makes concepts or ideas clear. Puttenham (*Arte*, p. 143) compares *energia* with *enargia*. *Enargia* gives "glosse onely to a language"; it exploits those qualities in words which have auditory appeal. *Energia*, on the other hand, is designed to give "efficacie by sence"; it serves "the conceit onely." In other words, *energia* is conceptual clarity in language; a clarity which can result only from the poet's precise apprehension of his own "fore-conceit" (see n. 62, above).

[427]Sidney was not alone in his hostility to affected eloquence and foreign vocabulary. See R. F. Jones, *The Triumph of the English Language* (1953), ch. IV.

[428]Sidney is attacking the excessive use of alliteration. Gascoigne (Smith, I, 47) makes a similar point: "For it is not inough to roll in pleasant woordes, nor yet to thunder in *Rym*, *Ram*, *Ruff* by letter (quoth my master Chaucer)."

were only peculiar to versifiers, and had not as large possession
among prose-printers; and (which is to be marvelled) among
many scholars; and (which is to be pitied) among some preachers. Truly I could wish, if at least I might be so bold to wish
in a thing beyond the reach of my capacity, the diligent imitators of Tully and Demosthenes[429] (most worthy to be imitated)
did not so much keep Nizolian paper-books[430] of their figures
and phrases, as by attentive translation (as it were) devour them
whole, and make them wholly theirs.[431] For now they cast sugar
and spice upon every dish that is served to the table, like those
Indians, not content to wear earrings at the fit and natural place
of the ears, but they will thrust jewels through their nose and
lips because they will be sure to be fine.

Tully, when he was to drive out Catiline, as it were with a
thunderbolt of eloquence, often used that figure of repetition,
Vivit. Vivit? Imo vero etiam in senatum venit,[432] &c. Indeed,

[429]Cicero and Demosthenes (384–322 B.C.), the Athenian orator, were
considered by many the best models for stylistic imitation, and their names
often appear together (cf. Smith, I, 8).

[430]Nizolian paper-books were named after Marius Nizolius, an Italian
lexicographer of the sixteenth century whose Ciceronian lexicon was widely
known. Sidney's contempt for collecting and copying phrases from other
authors, a process described and encouraged by Ascham (see Smith, I, 17),
results from his conviction that poetry should express unique personal feelings (see n. 425, above).

[431]Poets should read Cicero and Demosthenes for their wisdom and
learning, and not simply in order to collect elegant "figures and phrases."
The slavish imitation of Cicero's style was common in the Renaissance, and
earned the name of "Ciceronianism." Sidney's views on the matter are clear
enough in a letter to his brother (*Works*, III, 132): "I never require great
study in Ciceronianisme the chiefe abuse of Oxford."

[432]"The man lives. He lives? Indeed, and he even comes into the Senate" (adapted from Cicero, *In Catilinam*, I, i, 2). A similarly "well-grounded
rage" and doubling of words appears in Pamela's reply to Cecropia in
Arcadia (*Works*, I, 407): "But *Pamela* (whose cheeks were died in the
beautifullest graine of vertuous anger, with eies which glistered forth
beames of disdaine) thus interrupted her. Peace (wicked woman) peace, unworthy to breathe, that doest not acknowledge the breath-giver; most unworthy to have a tongue, which speakest against him, through whom thou
speakest."

inflamed with a well-grounded rage, he would have his words (as it were) double out of his mouth, and so do that artificially which we see men do in choler naturally. And we, having noted the grace of those words, hale them in sometime to a familiar epistle, when it were too too much choler[433] to be choleric.[434] How well store of *similiter cadences*[435] doth sound with the gravity of the pulpit, I would but invoke Demosthenes' soul to tell, who with a rare daintiness useth them. Truly they have made me think of the sophister[436] that with too much subtlety would prove two eggs three, and though he might be counted a sophister, had none for his labor. So these men, bringing in such a kind of eloquence, well may they obtain an opinion of a seeming fineness, but persuade few, which should be the end of their fineness.[437]

Now for similitudes[438] in certain printed discourses, I think all herbarists, all stories of beasts, fowls, and fishes are rifled up,[439] that they come in multitudes to wait upon any of our conceits; which certainly is as absurd a surfeit to the ears as is possible: for the force of a similitude not being to prove anything to a contrary disputer, but only to explain to a willing hearer; when that is done, the rest is a most tedious prattling, rather over-swaying the memory from the purpose whereto they were applied, than any whit informing the judgment, already

---

[433]"Anger," with a possible pun on "collar."

[434]Norwich: "too too much choler to be cholerlike."

[435]From the Latin *similiter cadentia,* "similar cadences." The term describes the rhythmic effect achieved when consecutive sentences or phrases terminate with the same cadence (e.g., "he who works heartily, works worthily"). It can also mean "rhyme." See Cook, pp. 127–28.

[436]A deceiver; one who makes use of fallacious arguments.

[437]"How well . . . their fineness": this passage appears only in Ponsonby.

[438]Similes; comparisons.

[439]Sidney is attacking the stylistic habits of John Lyly (died 1606) and his imitators, the "Euphuists," whose prose is well described "a surfeit to the ears." The style is characterized by alliteration, antithesis, balance, and an endless selection of images drawn from the animal kingdom. See *Astrophil and Stella,* III (*Poems,* p. 166).

either satisfied, or by similitudes not to be satisfied.[440] For my part, I do not doubt, when Antonius and Crassus,[441] the great forefathers of Cicero in eloquence, the one (as Cicero testifieth of them[442]) pretended not to know art, the other not to set by it, because with a plain sensibleness they might win credit of popular ears; which credit is the nearest step to persuasion; which persuasion is the chief mark of oratory;[443] I do not doubt (I say) but that they used these knacks[444] very sparingly; which, who doth generally use, any man may see doth dance to his own music, and so be noted by the audience more careful to speak curiously[445] than to speak truly.

Undoubtedly (at least to my opinion undoubtedly) I have found in divers smally[446] learned courtiers a more sound style than in some professors of learning; of which I can guess no other cause but that the courtier, following that which by practice he findeth fittest to nature, therein (though he know it not) doth according to art, though not by art: where the other, using art to show art, and not to hide art (as in these cases he should do), flieth from nature, and indeed abuseth art.

But what? methinks I deserve to be pounded[447] for straying from poetry to oratory:[448] but both have such an affinity in this wordish consideration, that I think this digression will make my

---

[440]Similes and comparisons add nothing to the substance of an argument, but simply make the ideas of the argument accessible. Accordingly, when a statement is already clear, the addition of "similitudes" is unwarranted.

[441]Marcus Antonius (143–87 B.C.) and Lucius Licinius Crassus (consul in 95 B.C.) were distinguished Roman orators and statesmen.

[442]*De Oratore*, II, i, 1 ff.

[443]Sidney's argument derives from Aristotle, *Rhetoric*, II, 1.

[444]The word "knacks," which appears in both Ponsonby and Norwich, has here been substituted for Olney's "tracks." The variant, which was understood to mean a "trick" or "cunning device" during the sixteenth century, is more appropriate in the context of Sidney's argument.

[445]Elaborately.

[446]Slightly.

[447]Impounded, as a stray animal.

[448]The association of poetry and oratory was common in the Renaissance because the disciplines had a common theoretical basis in rhetoric.

meaning receive the fuller understanding; which is not to take upon me to teach poets how they should do, but only, finding myself sick among the rest, to show some one or two spots of the common infection grown among the most part of writers; that, acknowledging ourselves somewhat awry, we may bend to the right use both of matter and manner; whereto our language giveth us great occasion, being indeed capable of any excellent exercising of it. I know some will say it is a mingled language.[449] And why not so much the better, taking the best of both the other?[450] Another will say it wanteth grammar. Nay truly, it hath that praise, that it wanteth not grammar:[451] for grammar it might have, but it needs it not; being so easy of itself, and so void of those cumbersome differences of cases, genders, moods, and tenses, which I think was a piece of the Tower of Babylon's curse,[452] that a man should be put to school to learn his mother-tongue. But for the uttering sweetly and properly the conceits of the mind, which is the end of speech,[453] that hath it equally with any other tongue in the world; and is

[449]"Mingled language" is a combination of two or more distinct languages. It was a common objection among the Elizabethans that the mother tongue was inadequate; either because the native vocabulary made clarity, or eloquence, impossible, or because grammar and spelling were insufficiently standardized. See R. F. Jones, *The Triumph of the English Language, passim.*

[450]Sidney is probably referring to Latin and Greek, though Latin and French is also a possibility.

[451]With the mounting prestige of the vernacular, which was encouraged by the Puritans and the Ramists, the development of an English grammar became a pressing issue. Many joined Sidney in praising the relative simplicity of English grammar (cf. Smith, II, 288–89).

[452]Sidney is referring to the familiar Old Testament story. Babylon, the capital of Chaldea, was built on the site of the Tower of Babel, which had been constructed in a vain attempt to reach heaven. Angered, the Lord ordered the confusion of tongues. "Therefore is the name of it called Babel; because the Lord did there confound the language of all the earth" (Genesis 11:9).

[453]This was a familiar notion among the Elizabethans. See *Works*, III, 266–68; and John Hoskins, *Directions for Speech and Style*, ed. Hoyt H. Hudson (1935), p. 2: "The conceits of the mind are pictures of things and the tongue is interpreter of those pictures."

particularly happy in compositions[454] of two or three words together, near the Greek, far beyond the Latin, which is one of
the greatest beauties can be in a language.

Now of versifying there are two sorts,[455] the one ancient, the
other modern: the ancient marked the quantity of each syllable,
and according to that framed his verse; the modern, observing
only number (with some regard of the accent), the chief life of
it standeth in that like sounding of the words which we call
rhyme. Whether of these be the more[456] excellent would bear
many speeches: the ancient (no doubt) more fit for music, both
words and tune[457] observing quantity, and more fit lively to express divers passions, by the low and lofty sound of the well-
weighed syllable. The latter likewise, with his rhyme, striketh a
certain music to the ear; and, in fine, sith it doth delight, though
by another way, it obtains the same purpose: there being in
either sweetness, and wanting in neither majesty. Truly the
English, before any other vulgar language I know, is fit for both
sorts: for, for the ancient, the Italian is so full of vowels that it
must ever be cumbered with elisions; the Dutch, so of the other
side with consonants, that they cannot yield the sweet sliding
fit for a verse; the French in his whole language hath not one
word that hath his accent in the last syllable saving two, called
antepenultima; and little more hath the Spanish, and therefore
very gracelessly may they use dactyls.[458] The English is subject
to none of these defects.

Now for the rhyme, though we do not observe quantity, yet
we observe the accent very precisely, which other languages

454Compounds. Joseph Hall, V*ergidemiarum,* VI, i, 255–56, suggests that
Sidney was copying the French in his habit of compounding words (e.g.,
"well-grounded"), though there was an equally strong classical precedent.
See Cook's note, pp. 130–31.

455See n. 269, above.

456Olney reads "most," but the variant "more," which appears in both
Ponsonby and Norwich, is preferable.

457Both Ponsonby and Norwich read "time."

458A dactyl, composed of an accented and two unaccented syllables (e.g.,
fórmŭlăte), is obviously easier to produce in languages abundant with words
that have accented antepenultimate ("the last saving two") syllables.

either cannot do, or will not do so absolutely. That *caesura*, or breathing place in the midst of the verse, neither Italian nor Spanish have; the French and we never almost fail of. Lastly, even the very rhyme itself, the Italian cannot put in the last syllable, by the French named the masculine rhyme, but still in the next to the last, which the French call the female, or the next before that, which the Italians term *sdrucciola*. The example of the former is *buono, suono*; of the *sdrucciola*[459] is *femina, semina*. The French, of the other side, hath both the male, as *bon, son*, and the female, as *plaise, taise*. But the *sdrucciola* he hath not: where the English hath all three, as *due, true; father, rather; motion, potion;*[460] with much more which might be said, but that I find already the triflingness of this discourse is much too much enlarged.

So that sith the ever-praiseworthy poesy is full of virtue-breeding delightfulness, and void of no gift that ought to be in the noble name of learning; sith the blames laid against it are either false or feeble; sith the cause why it is not esteemed in England is the fault of poet-apes, not poets; sith, lastly, our tongue is most fit to honor poesy, and to be honored by poesy; I conjure you all that have had the evil luck to read this ink-wasting toy of mine, even in the name of the nine Muses, no more to scorn the sacred mysteries of poesy, no more to laugh at the name of poets, as though they were next inheritors to fools, no more to jest at the reverent title of a rhymer; but to believe with Aristotle that they were the ancient treasurers of the Grecians' divinity;[461] to believe with Bembus[462] that they were first bringers-in of all civility; to believe with Scaliger that no philosopher's precepts can sooner make you an honest man than the

[459]"Slippery," referring to trisyllabic rhyme, as in *Old Arcadia*, VII (*Poems*, p. 14):

> Come *Dorus*, come, let songs thy sorrowes signifie:
> And if for want of use thy minde ashamed is,
> That verie shame with Love's high title dignifie.

[460]"Motion" and "potion" are pronounced as trisyllables.

[461]Boccaccio makes this point (*De Genealogia Deorum*, XIV, 8) and gives Aristotle as his source.

[462]See n. 362, above.

reading of Virgil;[463] to believe with Clauserus, the translator of
Cornutus,[464] that it pleased the heavenly Deity, by Hesiod[465] and
Homer, under the veil of fables, to give us all knowledge, logic,
rhetoric, philosophy natural and moral, and *quid non?*[466] to
believe with me that there are many mysteries contained in
poetry, which of purpose were written darkly, lest by profane
wits it should be abused;[467] to believe with Landino[468] that
they are so beloved of the gods, that whatsoever they write proceeds of a divine fury; lastly, to believe themselves when they tell
you they will make you immortal by their verses.[469]

Thus doing, your name shall flourish in the printers' shops;
thus doing, you shall be of kin to many a poetical preface; thus
doing, you shall be most fair, most rich, most wise, most all,
you shall dwell upon superlatives. Thus doing, though you be
libertino patre natus,[470] you shall suddenly grow *Hurculea
proles,*[471]

> *Si quid mea carmina possunt.*[472]

Thus doing, your soul shall be placed with Dante's Beatrix,[473]
or Virgil's Anchises.[474] But if (fie of such a but) you be born

[463] See *Poetices*, III, 19.

[464] Lucius Annaeus Cornutus was a Stoic philosopher of the first century
A.D. Conrad Clauser, a German humanist, brought out an edition of
Cornutus' *De Natura Deorum Gentilium* at Basel in 1543. Sidney here
alludes to Clauser's prefatory letter. See Shepherd, p. 236.

[465] See n. 13, above.

[466] "What not?"

[467] Sidney is offering one of the traditional justifications for allegory. In
his letter to Raleigh (prefixed to *The Faerie Queene*) Spenser describes his
major poem as "a continued Allegory, or darke conceit." Chapman takes a
similar stand in the prefatory letter to *Ovid's Banquet of Sense.*

[468] Cristoforo Landino was an Italian humanist of the fifteenth century
whose edition of Dante's *Divine Comedy* (first published in 1481) included
a preface with a section on "divine fury" (see n. 345, above).

[469] The "eternizing" power of poetry is a recurrent theme among Renaissance poets, though they were enlarging upon an ancient tradition.

[470] "The son of a freedman" (Horace, *Satires*, I, vi, 6).

[471] "Descendant of Hercules" (of doubtful origin).

[472] "If aught my songs can do" (Virgil, *Aeneid*, IX, 446).

[473] Dante encounters Beatrice in heaven in *The Divine Comedy.*

[474] Aeneas (*Aeneid*, VI) meets his father, Anchises, during his journey
to the underworld.

so near the dull-making cataract of Nilus[475] that you cannot hear the planet-like music of poetry, if you have so earth-creeping a mind that it cannot lift itself up to look to the sky of poetry, or rather, by a certain rustical disdain, will become such a mome[476] as to be a Momus[477] of poetry; then, though I will not wish unto you the ass's ears of Midas,[478] nor to be driven by a poet's verses (as Bubonax[479] was) to hang himself, nor to be rhymed to death, as it is said to be done in Ireland;[480] yet thus much curse I must send you in the behalf of all poets, that while you live, you live in love, and never get favor for lacking skill of a sonnet; and when you die, your memory die from the earth for want of an epitaph.

FINIS.

[475]Cicero (*Somnium Scipionis,* V) explains that just as the people who live near the Nile lose their hearing because of the furious roaring of the water, so men's ears are deafened by the music of the spheres (see n. 271, above).

[476]A dolt.

[477]Momus was the ancient god of mockery and censure.

[478]Ovid (*Metamorphoses,* X, 146–93) relates that Midas earned his ears by siding with Pan against Apollo in a singing contest.

[479]Cook (p. 133) suggests that Sidney has fused the names of Bupalus and Hipponax. Pliny (*Natural History,* XXXVI, v, 11 ff.) relates that Hipponax, a poet of the sixth century B.C., was publicly ridiculed for his ugliness in a statue by Bupalus and his friend Athenis. Hipponax secured his revenge by issuing poems so bitter that they were said to have driven the two sculptors to suicide.

[480]It was commonly believed that Irish sorcerers used charms to exterminate rats. Cf. Shakespeare, *As You Like It,* III, ii, 185.

Index